walking's new movement

opportunities, decelerations and beautiful
obstacles in the performances, politics,
philosophies and spaces of contemporary
radical walking

Phil Smith

(Crab Man and Mytho)

Published in this first edition in 2015 by:
Triarchy Press
Axminster EX13 5PF, England

+44 (0)1297 631456
info@triarchypress.net
www.triarchypress.net

A catalogue record for this book is available from the British Library.

Paperback ISBN: 978-1-909470-69-9
ePub ISBN: 978-1-909470-70-5
pdf ISBN: 978-1-909470-71-2

Printed and bound in Great Britain by
TJ International Ltd, Padstow, Cornwall

asking for directions

Over a period of a short few weeks, I listened to talks by Laura Oldfield Ford and Frédéric Gros and read a new book by Alastair Bonnett. My thinking about radical walking was shaken. For three months I walked and participated and watched and read and wrote. The shock to my long-held understandings and those three months of participation and reflection inspired me to identify and explain recent developments in the radical walking movement and to begin making a new context in which it might change again. To that end I propose here some massive practical projects, offer some smaller-scale tactics and promote a handful of new ideas.

I am looking with at least binocular vision, writing from within walking while simultaneously attempting an imagined helicopter or satellite view (the one de Certeau warned us against and Doreen Massey championed). I am trying to tease out the most progressive threads from the meshworks of walking, which means I have sided with some and against others. I have occasionally stuck my foot out in the hope of tripping up certain tendencies. I hope that the people I have criticised and those I have celebrated will understand that my arguments here are about ideas and practices rather than my feelings for them as individuals.

Something extraordinary has happened in radical and art walking in the last fifteen years, the work of many people and of many non-human forces, and this book is intended both to celebrate that and to furiously urge a new change and to help radical walkers realise it. I have attempted to provide arguments for such a change, a description of the necessity for it, models for some of the organising and thinking required for it and the first contributions to a new toolkit for producing it. More importantly, though, I have tried to sketch and gesture at the shapes, velocities and trajectories of relationships between people and things and ideas and spaces that might bring about the gyrations of a new orrery for a transformed walking.

Because I have favoured modelling these new trajectories in the spirit of exploratory ambulation rather than by listed demands or numbered manifesto points, you should be warned that, while I have tried to be direct and straight speaking, I have also sought to lure you into new trajectories by the curling and folding back of arguments and narratives. If conclusions come before arguments and interpretations before descriptions, then it is because that is how drift-thinking works. While everything may change, my impulse to wander without destination, in thought and body together, has not yet done so. Streams of thought loop back over the head of this plodding ambu-thinker; what is discovered up ahead as shiny and new has been documented at a stopping point left far behind. So, if I repeat myself, this may be my oblique way of getting at re-usable things; if I digress I may be avoiding the ironing out of wrinkles or the filling in of gaps.

Less admirable, but necessary to navigate, are the cultural and geographical limitations of my viewpoint manifest in omissions and biases.

Read this – partly map and partly muscle ache – as you might walk it; having arrived at where you don't yet know you want to get to, understanding that what you have walked best is where you must not go again.

1: threat

Things look pretty good for radical walking and for the latest generation of psychogeographers and walking artists. Don't they? After all, there are so many more of us doing this stuff than there were 15 years ago. Every now and again, someone high profile announces that the growth is over, walking's time has passed and psychogeography has outlived its purpose; everyone ignores them and our ragged-arsed juggernaut marches on. The flower keeps on opening wider. This growth affects other walkings too; the National Trust now organises barefoot walking on its paths, the Ramblers Association walks abject urban routes as well as country paths.

Yet the change and expansion is neither even nor simple. The performances of radical walking inside the expansion are shifting. Contradictory currents cross the zones of change. Some shifts begin as something simple and accumulative (more people doing certain things) and become changes of quality (all that extra doing changing the things done). General flows and tides emerge to show themselves: an increasing multiplicity of styles and means orbiting around a variety of ideas that together form and re-form approximate coherences; the growth in the number, visibility and influence of women walking, which in its turn exposes other and continuing absences; art and performance practices dispersing across the field; the return of romanticism and the attraction to 'new nature writing' within the prospect of an ecological catastrophe; the exposure of semi-hidden places of violence, intensification of the invasion of the subjective, the return of repressed legacies of psychogeography including iconoclasm and the occult; a renegotiation of the relation of theory to practice and the fraying at the edges of epic and sociable walkings.

3

Some of these changes may one day constitute potent problems for the multiplicities and transformational impulses that otherwise seem to bode so well for walking. For I have assumed for some time now that the explosion of walking arts, tartly and subliminally challenged as they are by intuitive sympathies for a political psychogeography with its roots in the early practices of the International Lettrists and Situationist International (IL/SI), are the right ingredients for a difficult, complex, savvy, corporeal, subversive, self-aware, increasingly post-dance-like walking, part of a broad and loose meshwork of resistant practices. My experiences while walking with some of those who are making this meshwork has only reinforced my optimism. At the same time, I have also begun to notice isolated events and actions that suggest that there is an accelerating discontinuity spreading across the field of radical, non-functional and art walking and I begin to wonder what, if anything, should be done about them.

Jenny Hughes, Jenny Kidd and Catherine McNamara have identified a moment in a process that they call "decomposition", when "designed and improvised.... processes deteriorate in confrontation with experiences that confound expectations of an orderly, rule-bound, habitable universe" (Hughes, et al., 2011: 188). Not for the first time I have been feeling that decomposition, experiencing it as a physical perturbation, as anxiety and queasiness, patches of dry skin opening into wounds; previously solid insights sliding into abjection.

During those three months in 2014, when I wrote and researched and visited and walked and re-wrote, in an attempt to orientate myself to a landslip I thought I had slept through, I began to remember things. Sometimes my reflections took me to dark places. Sometimes new research led me down among the minutiae of esoteric reports and arcane arguments. Yet even there, in darkness, dryness or obscurity, I found clues to something rich and treasure-like.

Part of what has emerged from this period of reflection and activity is a set of ideas for performing walking practices; some are original, others are hybrids or adaptations from existing practices. Taken together, they model performances of walking in relation to eco-romanticism, to misogyny, to occult ambiguity, to apocalypse, to

Savilian space and to the encoding of the city. They are a prescription for a new *dérive* that is already emerging, and has been for a decade or so now. Not quite David Bowie's "nine basic patents" in *The Man Who Fell To Earth*, but a start.

The results of my three months' thinking and doing are here and, if they are halfway accurate, they bode far better for radical walking than I had any right to expect when, rocked, I started out.

2 space wars

holey and hospitable spaces

There is a space war in progress. While there is private property and public space, of course there always will be. But it is not the fact of this war that is significant, it is the forms it is taking now and the terrains it is choosing, and where necessary, producing (war is as much production as destruction, hence its sustainability) for its battlefields. While the TV News may cover bombings at checkpoints, the 'taking' of this or that town, and the flight of refugees across borders, such violences are echoed in subtler, even invisible, changes of space elsewhere; the spectacle's encoding of everywhere.

Part of this space war, in bombs and code, is a battle for holey space, what Stephen Barber calls "city-space aperture[s] able adeptly to traverse all divisions between underground and surface, in order to instil its disruptive content into the relentless regulation of surface space" (2014, 90). This manifests at global and local scales, from the Israeli Defence Force's (IDF) attack on the tunnels of Gaza to the failed prosecution of Bradley L. Garrett and other place hackers (portrayed in some UK newspapers as unwitting wayfinders for terrorists) for accessing rail tunnels under London. But it is also an assault *on behalf of* certain uses of holey space such as air exclusion zones or the UK's Government Pipeline Storage System (ably monitored and critiqued by geographer Matthew Flintham).

Holey spaces targeted and defended include physical basements, silos, bunkers and hideouts, but also those invisible above-ground 'tunnels' we (and they) deploy for hiding in plain sight in the anonymity of city life. A radical walking can respond by accessing and keeping open some of the less vulnerable networks of holey space such as the trajectories of saluted magpies and imaginary sky creatures, processional walkways revealed by aerial photography, hollow lanes, and the encoding of spaces as pathways of joy and of night time revellers.

There are also ongoing changes to the space of gaze. Since the 1990s, radical geographers, activists and artists with an orientation to place have been engaging the monitoring of public spaces by CCTV. Now the first waves of outrage and novelty have subsided, the prevalence of the cameras is largely normalised in the UK and the authorities have moved on to securing spaces that are less vulnerable to visual surveillance – subjectivity, conscience and desire – targeted by a growing army of cognitive behavioural therapists who reconceptualise (and effectively so) their clients' thinkings, and governmental behavioural insights teams who, more unreliably, seek to value-add affect and motivation to the reception of government information.

One barely registers any more the request on the train to report "anything suspicious" to the guard. Immediately after 9/11 my local library (and, no doubt, numerous other publicly owned spaces) put up a poster advocating heightened public awareness of anomalies within the everyday; these tips for hyper-perception were uncannily like those for 'drifting'. In the space war our tactics are always, similarly, under threat of recruitment to an opposite purpose. Every new or adapted model that we devise will have been pre-empted or appropriated by the intelligence services' own version (although the IDF's purloining of *dérive* and flows – training their officers in the ideas of Debord and Deleuze – seems to have backfired on them in Lebanon, hence their recent reliance on bombing against Gaza) and likewise we should not feel inhibited about stealing our resources from our enemies' supply lines. (I did not call it 'Counter-Tourism' for nothing).

Complementary to the surveillance/spectacle's pincer movement beneath and within, is an ongoing assault on the hospitable upper surfaces of urban space. Any open green space larger than car-size will be ringed by protective boulders. The last remaining benches are disappearing from the suburbs. Imperative and prohibitive signs clutter everything. Where once there were generous urban shelters,

7

short and narrow shelves incapable of supporting a sleeping body predominate; 'designed' (in the sense of armed) to put any user in a state of tension, literally on the edge of their seats. The worker must work even in order to rest.

Only in the centres of a handful of cities are elegant architectural signature lines indisputable. The message is clear: there are now fewer valued spatial artists in the world at any one time than there are Ascended Masters. For everyone else there is aggressive visual incoherence and anxiety.

These are phases in a long process of re-spacing that discourages congregation and contemplation, subjects signs to an over-pixilation, strips human anomalies from public space in order to more starkly distinguish the suspicious from the harmlessly alienated and allows rich, affluent, comfortable, exploited, disturbed and poor individuals to move rapidly through central urban spaces without recognising each other. When André Breton famously claimed that the simplest of Surrealist acts would be to run down a crowded street firing indiscriminately into the crowd he assumed the crowd would be bourgeois. Today, bourgeois crowds hardly, if ever, assemble publicly. Part of the degrading of public space has been the disappearance from it of a bourgeoisie *identifiable as a class*; inhabiting a shadow space policed by private security firms, institutions and designers who carefully control and rent out limitation of access.

3: savilian spaces

There is in operation a dark version of the layering of space. Despite the queer and feminist deterritorialisations that an understanding of the relations between spatial layers can nurture and provoke, there are also reactionary reterritorialisations of such spaces, where the transitions and overlaps between the layers are exploited to make new spaces of violence, exploitation, threat and misery. This dark layering operates less across defined battlefields or in secret places, but more often alongside ostensibly benign and neutral spaces.

In the recent revelations about the abuse of vulnerable people, mostly young and mostly female, by celebrities, politicians and organised gangs in the UK, accounts of this abuse often describe a particular kind of space of abuse; a space that seems to have gone missing, become invisible or meaningless, that seems to have been largely unacknowledged in public, legal or academic discourses but to have been consistently exploited semi-publicly/semi-privately by abusers, both individual and organised, active in different class and cultural milieus.

In the case of the abuses of young women in Rotherham and other English cities, this Savilian space of abuse lies in a particular relation to family, 'community' and small businesses, in the same way as it has, in other instances, lain in a similar relation to the entertainment industry, churches, local and national state bureaucracies, hospitals, psychiatric wards and special schools. These Savilian places of abuse are often located somewhere between private and public space. They are places to which access is negotiated; though not public places they are usually 'known' to, even administered by, the institutions, families and communities the abusers operate within. These are not places of confinement or concealment, nor are they clandestine or taboo, covert or transgressive. They are inversions or inlets of semi-informal and semi-official space: dressing rooms, offices, private rooms on wards, curtained beds, and so on.

The behaviour of the perpetrators using such spaces is often described by witnesses as "reckless". But it is not unwitting. The late Sir Jimmy Savile, a TV personality and presently the most notorious individual associated with this abuse, would manipulate corpses into tableaus to which he was sole spectator and redeploy glass eyes as 'gemstones' for his finger rings. He did not hide his behaviour in a conventional sense, but performed an eccentric, sexualised presence, posing in skimpy clothes, leering through TV shows. Savile embodied the spectacle, but he also spectacularised embodiment: the body of no one – child, patient, elderly person or corpse – was safe from him.

So close at hand to an official world are Savilian spaces that these acts of apparent recklessness are in fact very effective in creating a symbiotic relationship between criminal and official spaces. Semi-hidden abuses in semi-hidden space put the official world in a position of 'semi-knowing'; hearing tales whispered behind the hand, gossip about 'bad reputations', and so on. By non-action and by witting, unwitting and half-witted collusion with abuse in a semi-public zone, powerful official bodies (hospitals, the BBC, churches, social services), consistent with what Slavoj Žižek describes as the ideology of all institutions ("pretend to deny your self-interest and you can have it all"), have legitimated outrages committed against some of the most vulnerable people in society.

The dynamic of this abuse has something in common with the pattern of anti-semitic pogroms described by Leon Trotksy in his book 1905 (1973). During these pogroms, the police would arrive, apparently to restore order, but then step back, allowing the mob to run amok. The violence of the mob would be legitimated by the semi-withdrawn passivity and disinterested witness of law officers (and often blessed by Christian priests). Pogroms so validated tended to be the most intensely violent of all. A more recent example of a similar dynamic would be the behaviour of Dutch UN peacekeepers and NATO forces at Srebrenica in 1995, first giving protection to Bosnian civilians and then withdrawing it, evacuating, witnessing and validating space for violence and exacerbating the mass murder of citizens by Mladić's Army of Republika Srpska and accompanying militias.

Savilian space is only different from these examples in that it is a semi-private space adjacent to public space, rather than public space itself, but it is subject to the same evacuation and validation (and to a greater or lesser extent the same disinterested witness) by official authority. Savilian space is a semi-privatised space within a public context, where abusive agents act with the accommodation, tolerance, connivance and embarrassment of public power and authoritative communal relations. These are places close to which authorities display their symbols, put up their signs, but then withdraw their responsibility and their empathy. A parade of authority and 'normal procedures' is followed by their effective self-negation, delivering a space where abusers are able to enact power and authority over victims in an apparently or semi-officially-validated, but evacuated, space. These are neither transgressive spaces nor 'temporary autonomous zones' but spaces validated by layers of a broader communal culture, ranging from a fearful not-wanting-to-know to an enthusiastic cheerleading, where Leeds football fans can chant in praise of Sir Jimmy Savile's rapes or where young women can be openly treated (and marked) by their communities as chattels unfit for agency in public space (with the embarrassed or pragmatic connivance of liberal authority). They are stages where the authorisation by, and then withdrawal or semi-withdrawal of, the state (or its surrogate authorities such as families or 'communities') empowers non-official individuals or groups to enact naked ideology and unapologetic power.

Part of the immunity of celebrity and political abusers was conjured by their performance of authenticity. Sir Cyril Smith, Sir Jimmy Savile and others were players in the sustaining of everyday Reality; they were bizarre and phantasmagoric expressions of

Ordinariness. Often with uneasy relationships to their working class backgrounds, the likes of Savile and Smith were best able to represent Ordinariness (and the freedom of opportunity to transcend it) by not quite ever being part of it. They were valuable ideological players in a fantasy about liberality and equality (behind which they, like other less-obviously rapacious manipulators, liberally took advantage of those less equal than themselves); further proof that without an understanding of the Spectacle one can mistake spaces of exploitation for those of liberation.

Sir Jimmy Savile crafted his control of space and spectacle as a Mecca(!) nightclub manager and DJ. He manipulated the adjacency of differently privileged spaces within a spectacular production of entertainment in which the main commodities were its consumers. He knew how to recruit wilfully 'ignorant' authorities to actively pimp for him; in 1967 town councillors of Otley (UK) paid for Savile's participation in a charity event by providing a tent of six young women overnight next to his own (Davies 2014, 236-41). Savile grasped quickly how liberalities could be engineered to generate their opposites, such as enforcement and silence. If Jack the Ripper was "probably psychogeographical in love" (i.e. in sexually motivated murder) according to the situationists (Andreotti & Costa 1996, 42), then Sir Jimmy Savile was certainly psychogeographical in rape. He self-consciously deployed what he called "the effect" to psychologically transform space, to create unreal places of invisibility and silence; as with the Whitechapel murders of 'Jack the Ripper' there was no irony or magic, only a dead-heart of misogyny-ideology (a discourse in which victims were always "it") beating down upon, and into, the unprepared.

If the UK government's 'Independent Panel Inquiry' (or something similar) into historic sexual abuse ever effectively reports, it may reveal something more than is presently known about the, possibly interwoven, roles of Savilian and related spaces (for example, private spaces of exploitation such as the guesthouses and flats that have figured in recent accounts of establishment abuse rings) in the processes of maintaining power, through the violent subjection of (mostly) young and (mostly) working class people and the blackmail of those in office by those in power. Part of any new movement in psychogeography, if any such thing is to genuinely exist as a force for change, might be an obligation to identify and classify in popular taxonomies the locations and general dynamics of these and other spaces of exploitative and repressive power, requiring an inquisitiveness every bit as un-tame as place hacking: "exploit[ing] fractures in the architecture of the city.... to find deeper meaning in the spaces we pass through every day" (Garrett 2013, 6). Alongside psychogeography's meanders, boosted by pleasure and affordance, this will be a harsh and threatened mapping. If we take it on, we should do so chastened by the understanding that reactionaries, with the advantage of hegemony, will be able to exploit our discoveries about transit and affordance while we can never re-utilise theirs about exploitation and repression.

The peeling away of psychogeography from general situationist theory (to which Stewart Home partly dedicated his *The Assault on Culture* [1991]), has in many ways released the *dériviste* from a burden of theory, but if we really want to engage with the exploitative power as well as the magic in the city, including the 'magic' of its exploitative power, then one of the tasks of the new psychogeographers will be to devise maps to locate, and toolkits to provoke, the textures and layers of the exceptional relations of the Spectacle in the same way as we have for the textures and layers of the spectacular Everyday. And Savilian space will constitute one of those layers.

Savile continues to be, like the murdering 'Jack', a malign force, but the two are very different. The Whitechapel murderer operated covertly, in the absence of witnesses and wreathed in mystery (to which others have been only too keen to add); Savile, on the other hand, could use space on the edge of observation, by exploiting the "effect" of the

Spectacle within such places to create opportunities to molest and rape. Savile's behaviour was a sick parody of psychogeography, he was adroitly aware of, and able to exploit, "the precise laws and specific effects of the geographical environment... on the emotions and behaviour of individuals" (Debord 1955/1981, 8). Psychogeography is still trying to get rid of the legacy of a late nineteenth-century psychopath; it needs to act quickly in regard to Savile and Savilian space before another reactionary mythos attaches itself to the movement.

Shifts in the nature of space challenge us to make new kinds of radical walking that take themselves more seriously as activisms against the Spectacle and against power. They challenge us to generate the movement (rather than 'create the organisation') capable of researching and sharing taxonomies of spaces of power, exploitation and affordance to freedom, exacerbating the pleasure we find in the free enchantments of everyday space and expanding the liberties we enjoy in holey space, while tracing, exposing and ending the abuses of Savilian and similar spaces.

This means more than a politics of everyday life; it means a politics *for* everyday life *as* politics, privileging everyday life as *the* site of politics *against* the discourses of the state and the agents of the Spectacle. Not a utopian politics of plans and visions, but an everyday political force working in the gaps "between 'art', 'politics', 'architecture', 'urbanism' and all the other specialisms that arise from separation.... to create a 'new' world where these specialisations will no longer exist" (Home 1991, 6).

What would that movement look like? What stories would such a movement tell itself and others? What dreams would it have, despite itself? What shapes would it form and what meshworks of structure and desire would it weave?

If the schizo-cartographer Tina Richardson is right (Richardson, forthcoming) and a 'new psychogeography' is now emerging in the UK, how will it deal with a part of its legacy from 'old psycho-geography' that might yet bring it down at its second step?

4: ripping yarn

The female walker faces the challenge to get beyond or around the threats that women face, in varying degrees, in public space. In conversations with women who walk considerable distances alone, like Alison Lloyd and Elspeth Owen, I have learned that even they are not inured to this threat but must skilfully manage and avoid it. They also have to get beyond or around imaginaries in which women are not agents in the landscape but figure *as* a landscape or as agents missing *from* it. At worst, women's bodies, both on the page and in the streets, are regarded as available to be landscaped, to be cut up and the parts assigned geographical significance. At a performance of Nando Messias's *The Sissy's Progress* which I attended in 2014 (more of this below) the audience were forcefully reminded of this when its procession accidentally tangled with a 'Jack the Ripper' tour guide.

The 'Jack the Ripper' murders have exerted a malign and grossly inflated influence upon the psychogeographical imaginary. The murders have long been aestheticised and mythologised: paintings by Walter Sickert are said to parallel the injuries and arrangement of the victims' bodies, ritual meanings have been attributed to the mutilation of the victims, and the 'power-magic' of a ruling class marking of space has been detected. Apart from the SI's own description of the never-identified murderer as "probably psycho-geographical in love", Alan Moore, a self-declared psychogeographer, has devoted an epic graphic novel, From Hell, to the myth.

Such is the level of psychogeographical fascination with this terrain and this set of murders, it is not surprising that Judith R. Walkowitz (1992) proposes that the flâneur figure itself emerged from a tradition of horror narratives and voyeurism that essentialises the walker as a male 'explorer' who reproduces the binaries of the city by retelling narratives of physical peril and sexual threat. By returning again and again to the 'Ripper' murders, male psychogeographers have perpetuated those binaries by leaping backwards over the Parisian *dérives* to their own misogynist genesis story, conceding psychogeography to an exclusively masculine agency. Here it is in remarkably bare terms articulated by Will Self: "men are corralled in this field due to certain natural and/or nurtured characteristics that lead us to believe – or actually do inculcate us with – superior visual-spatial skills to women" (2007, 12).

This is where Sinclair's direct line to "the ancestors" ("I'm actually having conversations with people who died forty or four hundred years ago…. it's a magical act" [Sinclair, in Hanson 2007]) crosses Richard Long's immersed progress across prehistoric Dartmoor; meeting at the head of a canonised procession from which women are almost entirely excluded; Robert Macfarlane managing to list just two women among his seventeen exemplary modern pilgrims (2012, 236-238).

It is from this procession that a 'new psychogeography*' must, painfully, detach itself, leaving behind some cherished sources, and find new precedents for itself (Margaret Cavendish, Charles Fourier or Nan Shepherd, for example), freeing itself from "the limitations of situationist psychogeography... ground[ed] in the male gaze" (Bridger 2013, 285).

(* I am taking the liberty, throughout this book, of purposely fuzzying the distinctions between psychogeography and other varieties of radical and art walking that are sometimes theorised, as in the case of Nick Papadimitriou's 'deep topography', Cara Spooner's 'greater choreography', Tina Richardson's 'schizo-cartography', Roger Bygott's 'integral drift' and the 'hybrid flânerie' of Bill Psarras, but not always; on the basis that what we still have to gain by further hybrids and overlappings is still far, far more than we have to lose by any fuzziness of definition.)

A recent attempt by psychogeographers to exorcise the 'Ripper' mythos illustrates the resilience of the problem. The Psychogeographical Commission has created a forty minute film, Jack the Ripper: The Banishing (2013), to accompany an attempted exorcism of the 'Ripper meme' involving actions at five Hawksmoor churches, invoking the pentagram-like arrangement of the churches as their "banishing" force. While the Commission's mash-up of Hammer and Hammer-like Ripper horror movies renders the imagery from the original films complex and layered, it still maps East London in women's blood. A détournement should depredate the parts from which it is constructed. Despite the film makers' best efforts, new registers of affect and symbolic meaning struggle to break from their originals, drawing upon an infection deep under the skin of psychogeography: images of fire light up depictions of the murders to the strains of melodramatic electronica. Jack the Ripper: The Banishing changes and challenges the meaning of the Hammer portrayals, but if anything, the visuals are reinvigorated rather than exorcised. The shortcomings of such a sophisticated attempt as the Commission's are a stark reminder of just how serious, and barely visible, are the consequences for a psychogeography that does not deal effectively with misogyny.

Bolstering and articulating the tradition of male domination in 'old psychogeography' is a very longstanding and resilient literary positioning of women in a landscape of passivity; this is just as common in past accounts by radical walkers as in those of more conservative literary walkers. In radical literature the landscape is female. The male walker explores the secrets of the landscape, often portrayed as someone seducing or penetrating a female entity. This trope was spurred by Thomas De Quincey and his wanderings "through the mighty labyrinths of London" in search of a fifteen-year-old prostitute, the objectified positioning of women in Breton's *Nadja* and Aragon's *Paris Peasant*, the tramper Stephen Graham's "making a sort of virginal way across the world" (1929, 51), Julien Gracq's descriptions of a city which "just like a woman – tightened the threads spun by our daydreams around herself, and better adapted the rise and development of our desires to her rhythms and moods" (1985, 2), Walter Benjamin's characterisation of the flâneur as less a philosopher-walker and more a "werewolf restlessly roaming a social wilderness" (1999, 418), Iain Sinclair's opening of *Lights Out For The Territory* with his notion "to cut a crude V into the sprawl of the city", and Debord's film Society of the Spectacle with its "subtitles [that] read 'We few, we happy few, we band of brothers'... Alongside the soft porn representations of women" (Tompsett 1995, 85).

It is hardly surprising, then, that a critical geographer like Doreen Massey might mistakenly conflate such a psychogeography with a parody of urban exploration to excoriate "the least politically convincing of situationist capers – getting laddish thrills (one presumes) from rushing down dark passages, dreaming of labyrinths and so forth. (Is this not itself another form of eroticised colonisation of the city?)" (2005, 47).

In art walking and radical walking there have always been women, often unrecognised. Women participated in the International Lettrists' and situationists' drifts, recent scholarship doing something to return them to visibility, though even their own accounts sometimes portray them more as spectators than agents: "went on a *dérive*... [W]ith Debord... he would explain the surroundings and the experience" (de Jong 2011, 187). The tendency of most journalists and some academics to repeat each other's stories – accounts of art walking that never get beyond Long and Fulton, accounts of the Situationist International that stop at Debord (now wholly unforgivable since the work of Simon Ford [2005] and McKenzie Wark [2011, 2013]) – not only excludes the majority of walkers but has exacerbated the deletion from public memory of women's immersion in walking.

The virulent ubiquity of this memetic war on memory and agency can be seen in the way that even a feminist critic like Elizabeth Wilson struggles to free herself from it in her influential *The Sphinx In The City*. When she describes how "[O]ne effect of the anonymity of the great city was that women became more vulnerable to the 'male gaze'. More generally, the condition of women became the touchstone for judgements on city life" (1991, 27), she is subject to a regressive looping of the spectacularisation of women with the critical generalisation of women-as-touchstones, a vicious cycle that entangles the patriarchy of the city with any critique of it, so that criticisms of the city (of its dangers, exploitations, violences, and so on) feed cycles of exclusion, privatisation and domestication.

What does, however, now seem to be breaking the fear of the path, and at the same time, at least among radical and art walking practitioners, dispelling the invisibility cloak, is the sheer exponential growth in numbers of women practising some kind of radical or art walking. It is the walking of actual women, following no particular manifesto (see Heddon & Turner, 2012), that is shifting the ground away from under the malevolent gaze.

We need to keep telling this story; to ourselves and to everyone else. A handful of years ago I was present at an academic conference where a male academic, bemoaning the absence of women in psychogeography, had to have it pointed out to him that all three of the session's panel members were female psychogeographers. As late as 2007, in the newsletter of the Centre for Urban and Community Research, Steve Hanson could ask of the male domination of walking: "[W]here are the female Psycho-geographers to subvert all of this?" (12) and, in answering his own question, list only one woman – a female academic who had "done much to re-gender the flâneur". In 2014, I was able to fill three pages of On Walking with the names of women walkers with connections to ambulatory arts or activism, and still, stupidly, manage to leave out Laura Oldfield Ford and many others. This reflects how things have changed rather than any virtue on my part, but unless we keep telling this story, and asking "what is becoming right with this picture?" we will again be subject to strange forgetfulnesses and partial visions.

We should not be complacent about the institutional and misogynistic siphoning and tunnelling to which walking has been subjected. However, though they may have distorted representations, they have so far demonstrably failed to halt the growth in numbers of women walking as part of an arts or psychogeographic practice. Indeed, a comical complementary relationship seems to have developed between this growth and the accelerating pace of predictions of psychogeography's demise by male practitioners including Iain Sinclair and Alastair Bonnett: what they really intuit is not the end of the *dérive*, but rather the demise of male-dominated psychogeography (while staking a claim to proprietary authority over its destruction).

When Tina Richardson, independently of the research here, proposed in 2014 that there was now a "new psychogeography", she presented a table of opposing elements ("What is it? What isn't it?"). Among the elements on the negative side were "Masculine/colonial", "Singularly literary" and "Univocal", among the positives was "Post-Sinclairian"; she seemed to be saying, in hope as well as analysis, that while a generation of male literary psychogeographers would not be forgotten, they would be superseded, as *the precursors to, rather than the originators of,* a new psychogeography.

5: the return of art through performance

When Fabian Tompsett characterises Debord's movie Hurlements en faveur de Sade (1952) as "a ludibrium, something he would latter (sic) theorise as 'creating a situation'" (1995, 83), he deploys a concept that may help us make sense of what is emerging, self-consciously and unplanned, from ambulatory arts. Tompsett illustrates the concept of ludibrium with reference to the origins of the Rosicrucian Order: an 'historical' account of the Order's activities had appeared in print some time before an actual Rosicrucian Order was formed. In other words, a fiction of an organisation brought a real organisation into being. Tompsett calls this a "drama with a project of social transformation" (83). The intention of such dramatic ludibria, made up less of dialogue and stage directions, and more of actions and provocations, is, on the one hand, to undermine any critical denial (that would, by definition, be false; there being nothing to deny), and, on the other, to let loose a fictional narrative and a dramatic world that invites its realisation in practice in the real world. It is a fictional score to be brought to life not by actors playing parts, but by its characters emerging from real life.

In the 1990s, Tompsett, Stewart Home and others attempted, not very successfully (and possibly not very seriously), to loose such *ludibria* on the world in the name of the London Psychogeographical Association (LPA). They issued critiques of the rituals of ruling class power, both abstruse (blood sacrifice) and overt (road building), and described in wishful terms the resistance to it: "huge gatherings of urban tribes bent on emotionally remapping the cities in which they dwell"

(Home 1997, x). The LPA's missives, swinging around narratives of *dérives* conducted to research the traces of ruling class powerplays in the landscape, continued a longstanding tradition of 'dark comedy'. These were invitations to actions for which there were few actual guests; because most other psychogeographers had no idea what they were doing or how different what they were doing was from their own activities. "[W]e had some things in common with them in terms of political background" a member of the Manchester Area Psychogeographic suggested, more in hope that understanding (Dickinson undated). In fact, they had almost nothing in common. Iain Sinclair was much closer to the mark when he referred to the LPA's "re-branding" of psychogeography as a "franchise" that "became a bit of a monster on the back of that" (Sinclair, 2002). That "monster", now fallen and decomposing, provides us with a rich and dispersed ground, long escaped from its franchise, and now open to all sorts of adventures, aesthetics and misuses as "[F]rom the 1990s activity among these revolutionary groups diminished and interest in psychogeography passed to the arts community (where it remains vigorous)" (Bonnett 2009, 60).

SWIM, Amy Sharrocks. Photo: Ruth Corney.

Not by any means do all walking activists and artists engage with psychogeography, but the abject and decomposing monster is still there to be remoulded; maybe, Golem-like, set to new tasks (with the potential, one hopes, for some uncontrolled outcome). While the 'real' Golem had the Ghetto to defend we have only a minor legacy. While a tiny handful of contemporary orthodox situationists may lament the rigourless dilution of SI theory, multiplicity makes fertile grounds for exchanges of *ludibria*, journeys through metaphorical terrains, volatile sites of contestation, and inner landscapes; Blake Morris's memory palaces, Jess Allen's *tilting@windmills* around the wind farms of Wales, the meditative procession of Robert Wilson, Theun Mosk and Boukje Schweigman's *Walking*, the collecting, carrying and passing on of precious objects by Elspeth Owen, and so on: "[T]he search for tactics, spatial practices and modes of expression with which to explore urban culture is leading to an increasing turn to work traditionally associated with the creative and performing arts and with the inventiveness of activist groups" (Pinder 2005, 387). That theatre in art, once so despised by hardline modernists like Michael Fried and Clement Greenberg, has prevailed in walking.

But is a multiplicity of practices enough? Today among radical walkers, perhaps as a reaction against past obscurantism (and occasional authoritarianism), there is little discussion of strategy. Perhaps that discussion is unnecessary? Even undesirable?

In the mid-2000s, site-artists Wrights & Sites demonstrated that something like strategy could emerge from tactics, when they suggested melding situation-making with *dérive* to make a walking that could *in itself* change the city. Wrights & Sites attacked the usual functionalist role of the *dérive*, a gathering of information about affordant spaces in order to make 'situations' (located events that defy the present economic and political system and prefigure a new kind of society). They moved beyond Debord's "double meaning: active observation of present-day urban agglomerations and development of hypotheses on the structure of a situationist city" (1981b, 39) to a third meaning, closer to the spirit of the *permanent dérive* in Ivan Chtcheglov/Gilles Ivain's famous 'Formulary For The New Urbanism' (1953), which might resolve the tension between Lefebvre's "moment" as it arises and the longevity of the "situation".

They proposed collapsing the walking into landscaping, taking from Michel de Certeau his empowering of pedestrianism, but getting beyond the structuralist passivity of de Certeau's everyday tactics by adding art-making without an aesthetic product; suggesting that performance and other arts practices could be integrated into situationist praxis on a walk in which the options, to perceptually reframe the city or to physically intervene in the city, were kept open. This had the advantage of change not being planned from above (which is a weakness of the situationists' urbanism), and instead coming by exploration and jouissance (intense pleasure) on the ground. The meanings of a place could be transformed in the process of 're-discovering' and re-enacting it and, when necessary, re-constructing it. In effect Wrights & Sites had invented a new drift-as-ludibrium: a 'situational *dérive*'. The touchstone of this 'situational *dérive*' is the whole-body jouissance of the walker, the city defined by the pleasure of a walking body; hypersensitised and micro-architecturally agentive; a prefigurative activity for a 'jouissant city'; a ludibrium awaiting a walking movement capable of fully enacting it.

When in 1998 Alastair Bonnett referred to the "failure" of the situationists to "effectively distance[d] themselves [from the] happenings and neo-Dada movements of the 1960s" (1998, 8), he identified a crucial silence in the SI's work: "the situationists hadn't developed an approach to creativity that did without the legacies and ideologies of artistic production... an approach that abandoned avant-gardism and made itself vulnerable to everyday struggle. More specifically, they didn't engage or research the myriad ways people explore and mutate their urban environment" (9). It is exactly this kind of "approach" that characterises the creative activity around walking today (largely developed since Bonnett was writing); the sources of that approach are a loosely meshed and at best vaguely psychogeographically-informed array of artists and post-artists, quite capable of negotiating (if not always successfully) the dematerialisation of the art object, relational aesthetics and post-dramatic performance. It is a commonplace (taken from live art, postmodern dance, spatial practices, art mapping, and so on) for these artists to place themselves in the junctions of art and the everyday, more oriented to deferral from, than refusal of, art. They tend to make "invitations to spend energy [rather] than spend money" (Bonnett 1998, 8), to share specialisms and the facility of technique in relational exchanges and are more likely to release their activities into the everyday than in a gallery or onto a theatre stage.

Ambulatory artists and activists engage with the ways in which environments are both explored and mutated in a walk; while sometimes fragmentary, these contemporary practices are parts of something similar to the ludibria of Home and Tompsett, but more welcoming to the uninitiated, grasping the provocative qualities of a teatrum mundi or of 'a game of war', yet working more often in a vernacular register than in poeticised theory or abstruse symbolic mapping. Where today's practices might occasionally spill over into opportunism or un-theorised spontaneity, walking might, equally well, suddenly spill over into dance; far better that, then, than to realise rationally and wholly (as localism or obscurantism does) some detail of a scenario that short circuits the 'ideal-entire' by giving credibility either to pragmatic things only or to the making of values by the exclusion of others from them.

In response to the problems of an ideologically marinated everyday and an inadequate situationist iconoclasm, Alastair Bonnett adroitly characterised the challenge to the contemporary *dérive* as "the problem of everyday creativity" (9). Recourse to de Certeau, the usual response to questions of the everyday, is of limited help; de Certeau's faith in the efficacy and effectiveness of walking as transforming the city's everyday is based on a questionable linguistic theory that perpetuates divisions of time and space, and of tactics and strategy, and between resistance in action and structures of power. Doreen Massey some time ago argued that, as a result of these binaries, "central power is understood as removed from 'the everyday'" (Massey 2005, 47) rather than the machinations of power being revealed for how they reproduce and maintain it in the everyday.

The serious theoretical consequences of de Certeau's complacency (and it is remarkable how often he is marched by psychogeography's writers in an apparently seamless procession with Dadaists and situationists, a procession that has become almost as predictable as that romantic literary one articulated by Marples [1960], Solnit [2000] and others) are at least twofold: firstly, an indiscriminate celebration of inequalities in supposedly 'rebel' forms (so "the Salvadoran or Guatemalan selling oranges on the freeways of Los Angeles becomes a figure of 'resistance'" [Ross 1996, 71] rather than an exploited worker without even the most basic rights) which drags psychogeographers into cheerleading for localism and neo-liberalism at the local level, and, secondly, an aversion to strategic thinking. As a result anodyne passivities and commercialised shocks can swamp the *dérive* and render it entirely incoherent. At the same time a lack of strategic thinking can lead to genuinely effective tactics becoming repetitious and unhinged from addressing the shifting structures of power on the streets. A schism then opens up in the *dérive* between tactics and strategy and the diverse results of that can include anti-political practicalism, a competitive disruptiveness for disruptiveness's sake (accompanied by anti-intellectual moralism) and the privileging of a literary account of a city that is structurally magical and self-reproducing.

Yes, difficult, isn't it?

So, if we are honestly looking for ways to do that difficult thing and interweave tactical activity with strategic effects, then Henri Lefebvre, for a while a confidant of the SI, may, even now, be a helpful guide for us. While Lefebvre tended to approach the everyday as something possible to characterise generally, as a readily available source of potent vivacity, he did not characterise this potential as a recuperation of a lost authenticity (though he believed the everyday had been eroded and underdeveloped, particularly in relation to technological development); rather, he described the everyday as realising its potency in an 'art of living' (Lefebvre 1991a, 213, also see Smith 2012, 168-9), entailing both "the disappearance of the divisions between superior and inferior moments of life, between the rational and the irrational; and between public and private" (Jappe 1999, 77) and a 'new wisdom', a lay wisdom of the ordinary that would be as sophisticated as the technical learning required for complex science and quite different from the 'great ideas' of philosophy.

Lefebvre argued for the efficacy of a "revolutionary romanticism" (the subject and title of a 1957 lecture by him), but it was in the everyday rather than in nature that he saw this romantic impulse realised, in the future not in nostalgia; a very different romanticism to that of the melancholic philosopher of walking Frédéric Gros, who claimed during the Q&A after his talk to the 2014 Bristol Festival of Ideas that "the memories of the walk are better than the experiences of the walk itself". Lefebvre's revolutionary romanticism has been characterised by Anselm Jappe as a "standpoint of the everyday.... [from which] everything that claims to be superior to it can and must be rejected, and this even within the sphere of revolutionary politics, including 'great' leaders, 'historic' acts, appeals to the eternal" (1999, 80).

If I can give an inadequate example from my own recent strategic fumbling to illustrate how this approach might be applied: I have become worried that I have sometimes over-emphasised seeking wonders in the everyday (with its own problems, 2014b) at the expense of exposing the oppressive homogenisation, fragmentation, marginalisation, policed containment and repressive incoherence inflicted on people in public space. (I have no wish to speculate on people's inner lives, which may be rich, deep and various, though it is hard to believe that these are enriched by the present politics of public space). At the same time I have no wish to leave behind my wonder-tactics for "a folk politics of localism, direct action, and relentless horizontalism" (Williams & Srnicek 2014, 354). My attempt at a response, following Lefebvre's model of revolutionary-romantic strategy, is to plan a distribution of alternative codes to the common things, signs, patterns, flows, encounters, and so on, in everyday public space. (This was partly inspired by conversations with painter and film maker Helen Billinghurst on a walk around Torquay and with the choreographer Melanie Kloetzel during experiments in protecting and developing subjectivity through 'common dance').

First identifying the ways in which these public spaces are constructed and rearranged as means to inflict codes that are both limiting, tedious and disorienting, I then assemble a taxonomy of things, patterns and so on through which these ideological processes operate in a particular public space. In response, I then create a series of new codes that might be obscene, poetic, dream-based, animal, utopian, philosophical, and so on. I then place this re-encoding on the buildings in these spaces, record their placing and distribute this information; so, now, the built environment can be read by others as a series of subversive and anti-ideological mnemonics.

A mythogeographical sensitivity to wonders (Smith 2014b, 4-6) can provide us with sufficiently anomalous architectures, textures and symbols for our "*imagines agentes*" (the material hooks in the built and natural environment on which we hang our ideas [O'Rourke 2013, 112]). This is a mapping of rebel ideas, dream theories and pleasure principles onto the built environment; an environment that is, of course, always changing and thus itself would be always finessing the codes, and helping to conceal their meanings from those who think themselves above going down into the streets to read the changes in the art of memory there.

Is this not what occult psychogeography, in its literary forms at least, has already almost done, by providing the scripts for an "attempt to participate vicariously in its [modernity's inhuman motor of transformation] positive feedback loop by fictioning or even mimicking it" (Mackay & Avanessian 2014, 36) and the raw materials for acts of subjective life capable of a "spirit of... endless inquiry and unbounded optimism and spontaneous delirium" (Radcliffe 2005, 327) without which the social part of revolution, or indeed activity of any kind, is without meaning for psychogeography. Here is an art of memory for anywhere, education without system; inscribing simply-reasoned radical and vitalist theories into the fabric of things, transforming everyday life into a giant *ludibrium*.

Part of the strategic virtue of such a project, at a time of increased global surveillance, theocratic government, private and state security, and the commercial corralling of behaviour, is that once the codes and arts have been devised, released and distributed in samizdat and rumour forms, those in central power will be unable to remove them or their architectural and everyday signifiers from an everyday invisible discourse without bulldozing the entire everyday world. Those reading the codes in the everyday will learn how to do so without outwardly signalling their finessing of their mind maps (dancing with their eyes only). There is nothing especially new about this; except the people who will be doing it is this time. Ruling classes have for a very long time communicated secretly in plain sight; think heraldry, neo-classicism, haute couture and so on.

Here then is a strategic deployment of performance-like tactics that is not realised in art, but in everyday walking through everyday space, enabled by aesthetic technique but without aesthetic product, "a direct organization of higher sensations" (*Internationale Situationiste*, 1/21, 1958, 90, cited in Jappe 1999, 79), dematerialising art and reconstituting it as something else, drawing on the dynamic of performance but not its contemporary tendency to favour other performers over the audience of strangers.

I do not suggest for a moment that this answers any questions about future strategy for a 'new psychogeography' or the radical walking movement, but I think it might be a model for something more than a single project.

6. walking with nando

The Sissy's Progress is an ambulatory artwork made by performer and queer academic Nando Messias in response to a homophobic assault suffered close to his home in East London. It begins in a closed and crowded space with an invited audience. Messias is naked except for make-up, jewellery and heeled shoes; he puts on a bright red dress and engages in ambiguous rituals with performers dressed as suited 'City brokers'. Then, in the second phase of the performance, these performers become a marching wind band and Messias processes out of the closed space into the streets, with his audience walking in procession.

The performance blends elements of vulnerability and display; Nando seems more naked dressed on the street than unclothed in the enclosed space. The procession both dominates the streets and sets itself at the mercy of them. When I saw it, at one point on the route Messias stopped and the band fell silent – although there was no explanation, it was clear that this was the scene of the homophobic assault. Suddenly we were being harangued by an irate 'Jack the Ripper' tour guide, first about his right to do his tour despite us, and then with the grisly details of the mutilations suffered by a woman murdered at this site in 1888: "right where that bloke in the dress is!" The tour guide finally led his group away, and our procession set off again, attracting stares from passers-by, making its way uneasily through a crowd of City workers standing outside a pub and under the quiet and intrigued gaze of a second tour-guide party.

'The Sissy's Progress' by Nando Messias (2014).
Photo: Loredana Denicola

Back outside our starting point, a ritual of music and water was performed, both sinister and celebratory, a humiliating re-enactment of an assault and an exorcism of it.

This walk did not resolve the space of its streets, but provoked it to show its contradictions; the various layers of the route – most startlingly at the site of the assault – were set in motion by the performance putting itself at the mercy of them. There was no ideological standing above the situation, nor any semi-official personae straddling authority and transgression; there was only the 'to the side' (the non-literal, oblique angularity) of performance. No final, fixed, authentic, or 'real' places or meanings were revealed by *The Sissy's Progress*; the 'reality' of any one of them (their 'right' to exist, to be let alone, to be heard) was disputed by one or more of the others. There was no undisputed meaning, no secure space for identity-making, not even a reclaiming of the space from violence; all those things remained unresolved. What, instead, was revealed and celebrated/exorcised/invoked were the different spaces within the one space, no one of them more 'real' or authentic than any of the others; different strata of conflicting personal and cultural performances and displays, layers of violence (both the history of violence, but also the potential for future violence in the coldness and aggression of certain encountered gazes), different and conflicting narrations of the same place, all cutting through and across each other.

Rather than these layers comfortably meshing, as a somewhat idealist, pro-situationist approach to the city might suggest ("lives and activities intertwine... connections are made with stories that are interwoven" [Pinder 2001, 9]), Nando Messias's performance animated spaces that remained conflicted and tense, more like Chris Jenks's "minatorial geography.... exud[ing] not so much from the walls and pavements as from the encoding of selectivity, the interaction of suspicion and distance" (Jenks 2004, 41), and yet had positive dynamics, like those described by Gillian Rose as "paradoxical... spaces that would be mutually exclusive if charted on a two-dimensional map... [that] are occupied simultaneously" (1993, 140); spaces which, according to Kevin Hetherington, offer "possibilities of multiple positioning... [B]y attempting to act differently from social expectations, by being Other in the territory of sameness" (1997, 27).

In September 2014 I took part in a workshop on walking performance led by Nando Messias at the KARST studios in Plymouth (UK), as part of the Live Art Development Agency's DIY 11 scheme. The conclusion of the week's work was a showing of work-in-progress which demonstrated (at least to me) the rich potential of deploying multiple tactics sensitive to terrain, to layers, to planes, to rights, to gender and to appearance *if and where* there is a primary body-identity-provocation to shake the layers of that terrain. Performed on a plaza in Plymouth's busy city centre, this showing drew together different performances; for example, Jazz taking a plant for a walk, Veronica staging a picnic and leading her participants on a crawl, Debbie changing the frame of the space for invited guests. Alongside them, I tried to triangulate myself with the trajectory of any one non-human animal and of any one inanimate thing on the move; trying to broaden, fragment and give up parts of my own agency. Once a triangulation with animal and thing was achieved I would throw myself down onto bubblewrap and a piece of cardboard, on which I had written UTOPIA CLOSING DOWN (taken from the frontage of an empty shop), and spill the contents of a water bottle onto the pavement in an attempt to 'complete' the pattern of various spills of fats and other substances on the plaza's surface and reproduce the esoteric symmetries (feng shui and tree of life) informing the city centre's architect, Sir Patrick Abercrombie and his original plans for its redevelopment.

Throughout the showing, which lasted about an hour, I was repeatedly approached by passers-by who unpatronisingly asked me what I was doing. I explained about the esoteric symmetry of the city centre and my attempt to renew it; their responses to this were as serious as their enquiries and again and again I had to terminate our conversations in order to continue with my score. I had never experienced quite such a consistently serious and spontaneous engagement from passers-by nor such a feeling of comfortableness with what I was doing. I am convinced that this was not mostly down to anything on my part, but rather was chiefly effected by the body-identity-provocation performed by Rob, another of the workshop participants.

I had already sensed from *The Sissy's Progress* in East London, and then again when Nando, in make-up, walked side-by-side with each of us in turn around Plymouth city centre in a variation on the *Progress*, that there was an intensely-affordant destabilising of space in his performance of gender and feminine masculinity. I found both the *Sissy* performances mixed nervousness with euphoria, vulnerability with display. For our work-in-progress in Plymouth, Rob, in skirt and make-up, created the same productive and rich instability; he walked around the plaza hand-in-hand with one member of our audience at a time, either of them breaking their hands if they felt at any time that they were being addressed or gazed on in an aggressive or unfriendly way; not only performing a provocation, but also a response to any negative response, giving witnesses instant responsibility for their own reactions. I am as certain as I can be that our multiple disruptions of space, with Rob's as the key and indispensable motor (and I have no illusions that it comes at a cost and a risk to the person powering that motor), was what created eddies in the ideological and social space of the plaza, helped by the sweeping views across its expanse, and the paradoxically calm context for me to work in. Rather than disrupting the flows of the plaza alone, I could be a part of a contra-flow in which the binary of two sexes "cross[ed] over into molecular assemblages of a different nature... not only the man in the woman and the woman in the man, but the relation of each to the animal, the plant, etc.: a thousand tiny sexes" (Deleuze & Guattari 1998, 235).

I felt that we had found something, a certain model-like conflation of ideas and tactics, on that plaza. I was able to meet whatever the sum of that conflation was by moving abstractly in relation to pigeons and blown packaging – a shift to dance, a refusing to be scared of dance. I performed a "circulation of things, and of human beings trapped in a world of things" (Debord 1981a, 70). I performed these things not as commodities but as vibrant matters. I subjected myself (and performed/represented my subjection) to a combination of physical forces like those described by Debord and Jorn for their *The Naked City* map: "the slopes that naturally link the different unities of ambience; that's to say the spontaneous tendencies for orientation of a subject who traverses the milieu without regard for 'practical considerations'" (Jorn, 1985). This felt like self-organisation, something like the dynamic patterns (including basins of attraction) described by Kelso (1995), something like Nick Land's "methods that do not interpret assemblies as concretizations of prior theories" (Land 2011, 495) and something like finding a way to an anti-commercial, 'essential' city, subject only to "the drift's romantic, automatist undercurrent" [Sadler 1998, 91]). In the overlappings of our showing and the activation of the layers of the plaza, rendering separations at least supple if not breaking them down, and in my self-subjection to the abstract-physical pressures of commercial space and animal behaviour, I felt that we had found something like Nick Land's manoeuvres for a complex and multiplicitous dynamic patterning in engagement with multiple complex memes, 'other' than human consciousness yet patterning human consciousness, while engaging against the constructing of illusions of legitimacy. We had found a score that was "entirely intractable to subject/object segregation, or to rigid disciplinary typologies... no order of nature, no epistemology or scientific metaposition, and no unique level of intelligence" (Land 2011, 495). I was implicated and implemented.

By throwing myself into the horizontal, onto bubblewrap and cardboard, I found myself unexpectedly, momentarily, in tune with the anti-humanism of Nick Land, his idea of upright posture as a "calamity" and his advocacy for an "attempted recovery of the icthyophidian or flexomotile spine: horizontal and impulsive rather than vertical and stress-bearing" (501). I had (literally) stumbled across a de-normalising trajectory, from vertical to horizontal, to add, with difficulty, to nomadic thinking's walk away from sedentary thought.

7: war of selves

The struggle for the subjective in psychogeography is not an added bonus or a self-indulgence allowable once the serious business is complete; it *is* the serious business. The architecture of multiple selves rather than the architecture of the streets is the key terrain of psychogeographical change; nothing changes until we first realise, each one of us, that we are alone and that nothing changes unless we allow that aloneness to change it. Everything else – comradeship, violence, democracy, environment, ideas – is scaffolding. No wonder revolutionary capitalism is so indifferent to structure and so vampiric upon every *impulse* to create, every *desire* to produce and every *spirit* of enterprise.

Equally, though this struggle may be about subjectivity it is not about introspection. There are affordant and non-affordant material, geographical and social locations for this struggle for subjectivity, and the best are not always those we might expect. Isolated, hidden or obscured places sometimes offer least, while public places, with their apparent dangers of exposure and vulnerability – where gaps and differences, even tensions and conflicts, appear – are often the most fruitful places to "think beyond narratives of originary and initial subjectivities and to focus on those moments or processes that are produced in the articulation of cultural differences. The 'in-between' spaces provide the terrain for elaborating strategies of selfhood – singular or communal – that initiate new signs of identity and innovative sites of collaboration, and contestation" (Bhahba 1994, 1-2). We may be in a struggle to win our subjectivity back, but the consequences of succeeding do not have to include solipsism.

We have not been invaded by aliens, but by the techno-linguistic machines that constantly seek to know us. We are now in a war in which we are our own worst enemies; colluding in our own exploitation, labouring for those who do not pay us with every keystroke to social media, producing ourselves for consumption by ourselves. We must 'turn' and recruit ourselves as 'sleepers' in a new 'cold war', nurture dark and silent doubles, protecting our selves in darkness and embracing them to nothingness (to the despairing self-knowledge that only in aloneness we can change anything). There have been many 'last battles' and 'wars to end all war', but it is hard to know how much deeper than the hidden part of selves this threat can go.

We are in the midst of a guerrilla war for what people once called 'the soul', that properly dark and appropriately hidden part of you, a delicacy once hungered after exclusively by priests and false messiahs, but now desired by business and government just as much. Once upon a time acts of non-normative self-affirmation were accompanied by fear of exposure ('now the fascists knew where we were'); today, such exposure is translated into information currency in a digital marketplace. The performance that once disrupted and differentiated itself from the normative is made digestible.

In this fast war, in which information is exchanged at bewildering speeds, we will have to learn to be Schweikian walkers, playing stupid, slow and shallow, dancing subtly under our own clothes, forgetting to bring our devices, in the worst cases learning to dance with our eyes only, refusing so politely to be the producers of ourselves-as-commodities that no one notices, learning discretion, putting machines of invasion into reverse so they become the means of dispersal rather than exposure, seeking secret places of footfall for confession and intimacy; all these tactics have been prefigured in the intricacy, presentness and presence of live art or in those modern pilgrimages described by Robert Macfarlane (2012, 236-8) and others.

The work of the ideology-pilgrim is doubled, and then doubled again. It is not an initiation into mysteries hidden within, but, to begin with, a double journey, firstly through a real landscape saturated by ideology, a space where "virgin", "wild", "primal" and "unspoiled" are marks of fabrication (in both senses of nobly crafted and scandalously faked), where materiality cannot be relied upon as a counter to its own deceptions, and, secondly, a walk towards a revelation that is no more a given than the rest of the route, but is constructed and reconstructed by each journey, through "the necessity, the responsibility, to examine anew and to invent" (Massey 2005, 169); not a solipsist or spiritual journey to some 'revelation' about the self, other than revealing how much the self is implicated in making everything that imprisons it:

> "[L]ike the mysterious entity called 'I'... undetectable by ordinary instruments... it is possible to deny that Chapel Perilous is really there. And yet once you are inside it, there doesn't seem to be any way to ever get out again, until you suddenly discover that it has been brought into being by thought and does not exist outside thought." (Wilson 1978, 10).

Passing through the Chapel Perilous of any journey is not an escape from one space to another, but a choice between the obligation to reproduce the Chapel over and over again in the name of novelty – an occult or literary act that becomes stranded forever in its admiration of itself in the ornaments of the mysterious Chapel – and the obligation to walk-think-invent a space so artificially and self-consciously that the walker-consumer, by becoming walker-artificer (taking both Žižek's third pill to find not the reality behind the illusion, but the reality *in* illusion, and my fourth pill, to *make* a new fabrication), is brought to the door of the Chapel beyond which are spaces that do not exist yet and which (so is the lesson of utopia) are inhibited by description. *This* is how to do the 'situational *dérive*'.

The 'situational *dérive*' is a baroque form of walking. Unwilling to accept that "[D]emands for rights to the city... require the production of an appropriate space" (Pinder, 2005, 400), it is a rejection of conventional planning, even of the utopian 'New

Babylonian' kind, and instead prosecutes a conflation of walking and architecture; a re-making of the city's meaning through both spontaneous and choreographed walks armed with *détournement* and performance (Crab Man and Signpost 2012, Wrights & Sites 2006). Much still needs to be done to meet the aspirations of the 'situational *dérive*', but it does at least challenge a passive 'drift' that is forever putting off any 'situation'. While our prematurely forcing this issue here may smother some of the richness of the contemporary *dérive*, must we keep on repeating the present and comfortably prefiguring a future we do so little to usher in?

The responsibility to "invent" (Massey 2005, 169) can only be fulfilled by the irresponsibility of refusing to imagine even what contradictions or forces of production might power up such invention; imagination being the most saturated site of ideological reproduction. While there has been some exaggeration of the extent to which situationist urban plans like those of Ivan Chtcheglov/Gilles Ivain's 'Formulary For A New Urbanism' have already been realised parodically ("[L]iving in one's own cathedral', in the i-tuned virtual twenty first century city of individual ear-plugged bubbles, has become reality" [Skoulding 2012, 120]), in fact the real problem with such plans is not how they have been, but rather how they might have been realised: "[A]though the LI, and later the situationists, planned a *total transformation* of the urban environment, they never advanced a workable plan of how to maintain a sense of human community during and after this transformation" (Home 1991, 21).

Instead of drawing up plans, the 'situational *dérive*', whether an epic narrative wander or a disrupted trip to the shops, seeks to come repeatedly to the door of the Chapel Perilous and then refuses to step through to utopia; this is a new mental and physical architecture of deferrals and refusals, not constant freeflow but repeated portal-interruptions. Walking with a slippery mental panopticon of multiple doorways (the orrery brought to a new stage of dynamism), this mobility is interrupted and limited not by destinations and productions but by decompression chambers, vaults, airlocks and encounters. Pulling apart borders, fences and walls in order to construct beautiful obstacles. This is 'ambulatory architecture' as championed by Wrights & Sites.

Resources for such a practical and subjective architectural interventionism can be drawn from a certain kind of 'occult' psychogeography, exemplified, for example, by the London Psychogeographical Association's *The Great Conjunction* (1992), which combines astrological events, labyrinths and a narrative about substitute ritual murders sustaining the rule of the British royal family. It is a work of so elaborate and arcane a nature that it tests the most enthusiastic and esoterically informed reader. That is the point: this 'testing' is a part of its purpose – the text is a 'magical' work in itself. Unlike the softer, literary versions of occult psychogeography popularised by Peter Ackroyd or Alan ("magic... any cunt could do it") Moore, the LPA's difficult text 'magically' transforms (or repels) its readers through the very act of reading; the mind re-shaped by its negotiation of the labyrinthine text, encouraging a paranoid and hyper-exegetical reading sustaining multiple simultaneous connections. Or at least that seems to be the intention; in reality it probably needs rather a lot of help from a willing reader; nevertheless, this 'magical' reading is an attempt to both illuminate *and imitate* the baroque dynamics by which a ruling class prepares the ideological nexus for future transmutations: "[T]he psychogeographer who's prepared to open their mindset up to invisible forces can comprehend the mental, imaginary fields where the... landscape is being mapped" (MAP 1987).

Many psychogeographers have, not surprisingly, resisted all such 'occult' fancies; in practice and in principle. Some stick to Debord's hard line on irrationalism, repeating the situationist critique of surrealism ("over-reliance on the subconscious" [2005, 9]) and in so doing surrender the ground of interiority to others. One group, the Materialist Psychogeographic Affiliation (MPA), was founded in 2007 with the explicit purpose of eradicating occultism from psychogeography. The problem for such commonsense psychogeographers is that in place of the occult they have tended to offer a dull algorithm and an unremarkable localist reformism; in the case of the New York Psychogeographical Association a "clear sense of psychogeography as a constructive and engaged practice... increasing the number of bicycle lanes, expanding bus use" (Dusty Bin, 2000). Seeking a materialist dynamic to drive their project they fall upon alienation just as its nature shifts in response to the digital penetration of subjectivity: "[T]he dilemma that human beings must face in the twenty-first century is not that they're alienated or ignorant, but that they're not alienated or ignorant enough" (Guffey 2102, 8).

Those looking for a genuinely reactionary, nostalgic, irrational or gothic charge in psychogeography might do better to shift their focus from the rational/irrational and modernist/nostalgic binaries of occult psychogeography to those walkings that are normalising, that are proposing walking as a universal or equalising agency ("like all animals we leave tracks as we walk... 'Always, everywhere, people have walked'" [Macfarlane 2012, 13]) or to those psychogeographers who are selective about which histories and landscapes they want to address. When it is possible for innovative walkers to write that "[T]he Situationist dérive was a process heavily reliant on the depth of strata comprising Parisian psychogeography. Compared to the United States for example, where even east coast buildings are rarely more than a hundred years old" (Craig & Wilding 2005, 11), then it is clear that there are times when psychogeography has to unclip itself from architecture and physical trace and listen for the silence, feel for the absence, dream the trauma of colonial spaces.

This problem is spatial as much as temporal: "[T]he trouble with the Engenglish is that their hiss hiss history happened overseas, so they dodo don't know what it means" (Mr 'Whisky' Sisodia in Salman Rushie's *The Satanic Verses*). The malevolent wreckages of colonialism and misogyny are everywhere the far-reaching strata that are crossed by our drifts; material "depths" that may have to be accessed by ludicrous means. Recently I have begun to hear the voices of what I call 'street demons' (footings for temporary fences that look like howling faces) as articulating this ever-present colonial trauma, demanding a permanent state of recognition; in reality, they are (at least for me, and now they can be for you) metaphorical reminders of these traumas; something I first became sensitised to while walking and dancing with Melanie Kloetzel. Just as much as the *dérive* should be engaging with geological, ecological, vibrant material, non-human 'natural historical' and cosmological strata, so it should never seek to get away from just how compromised are its traditions: "North-West Passage"? Really?

Tying the 'drift' to a selective architectural heritage or to reforms of street furniture or to efficient and responsible traffic flow rationalises it just when what it needs most are the dynamic patterns and irrational forces of production of something like the 'Abstract Culture' of Nick Land and others. Otherwise the 'drift' is made hierarchical and subject to localised versions of an exclusive 'view from above' famously and decisively critiqued by de Certeau. What the contemporary *dérive* needs, disrupting that elevation from below, is what Steve Pile has called "the emotional work of city life. Dreams, magic, vampires and ghosts" (2005, 3). Rather than trying to imagine and realise an architectural *gesamtkunstwerk* like Constant's *New Babylon* or Chtcheglov/ Ivain's city of quarters, a new walking movement might appropriate the baroque style of occult psychogeography and begin to 'quietly' but publicly encode the existing city in an art of memory, making small material interventions where necessary to finesse the code, realising both Chtcheglov/Ivain's aim of a "baroque stage of urbanism considered as a means of knowledge and a means of action" (Chtcheglov 1953, 3) and Doreen Massey's dictum that "[W]e come to each place with the necessity, the responsibility, to examine anew and to invent" (Massey 2005, 169).

If the aim of psychogeography is for a city to "become a giant playground, its quarters acting as stations for a perpetual Revolutionary Festival" (Sadler 1998, 120), why expend energy on destruction and production when with little effort new opening and re-naming ceremonies might be performed, re-designating the function and meaning of places? A new ghost-architecture of psychogeography can start from what ambulatory arts can provoke, "the feeling that the smallest details and moments acquire new meaning as if in accordance to some strange pattern" (Pinder 2005, 397). Psychogeography can 're-shape' a city into "as if" patterns, using the template of 'occult' exegeses like *The Great Configuration* to attribute new meanings to both generic and unique elements of a city, rather as the Institute for Infinitely Small Things engaged with multiple lay authors to rename all the streets and squares of the city of Cambridge (Massachusetts) for their art-map *The City Formerly Known as Cambridge*.

To walk a city re-encoded would be a re-composition of that city's meaning; the shared code adding strategy to de Certeau's otherwise over-optimistic tactics, while the code's unfinished parts and ambiguities would always ensure that any reading was necessarily an active and compositional one. By writing and then refining the incomplete codes, the mostly unseen and undetectable process of de-composing and re-composing a city might predominate over any cod-sinister hiddenness or finality of meaning.

Emily Orley has, in another context, identified what the principles and tactical details of a "quiet" process such as psychogeographical coding might be:

"first we anthropomorphise place: that we literally regard it as having the human ability to 'do': to live, to grow and to remember... observe how it 'behaves' in the present time of viewing by bodily inhabiting the place and by being fully present in it... if the visitor... pays close enough attention, she can become aware of what (and indeed how) the place is 'doing' around her... The second stage of the method involves... the production of work that invites new encounters, that encourages new dialogues... So the ethical relationship fostered in stage one, becomes, in turn, the ground upon which creative action might be attempted" (Orley 2012, 42).

Without conceding anything to the supernatural this brings together the 'characterisation' of place (*genius loci*) used by the occult tendency within psychogeography (and by neo-romantics like Arthur Machen and Paul Nash upon whom it draws) with the turn to art in contemporary disrupted walking. By sharing and deploying decompositions and limited encodings of place through unprofitable 'art' (technique without product) the process can shift gear from subjective pleasure to a democratic 'art of memory' anywhere. To be effective would of course require a qualitative leap beyond what passes at the moment for representations of walked place and a strategy for laying various encodings over, under and around each other in ways that others could understand and commit to memory. Theoretical sophistication and (a sometimes sectarian) passion have proved no substitute for artistic technique divorced from art production: a code, a fanciful mapping that cannot be read except through another journey, a score that is only visible when performed.

Maybe this is a good time to activate those ludicrously crude ideas of Henri Bergson's (passed on by Gilles Deleuze) that the brain is a screen and the universe is meta-cinema, transforming them by a kind of tentacular spectatorship, eyes on stalks, seeking out cinema in the 'real world', to make good a political demand for 'a life like a movie' not by passive consumption but by senses-out walking that is simultaneously a staging, a tracking, an editing and a critical practice: "across and between film and performance, in intimacy and riotous contestation, through darkness and illumination: that unknown zone... where future histories of the human body will be generated and witnessed" (Barber 2014, 7).

If we add to this (it is already present in Orley: "[I]f place is a throwntogetherness, we are part of what is being thrown together" [40]) a conscious re-making of ourselves through an "understanding that regards the mythogeographer, the performer and the activist as being just as much multiplicitous and questionable sites as the landscapes they move in" (Smith 2010a, 115), "place and mind... interpenetrate[d] till the nature of both is altered" (Shepherd, 8), then we have both the pilgrim responsibility of our own agency ("a self as likely as any place to be 'just passing through'" [Smith 2003, unpaginated]) and the implicated/implemented duality of our relation to the 'other' close at hand (the extent to which we put ourselves on the line here is a partly chosen luxury [see Smith, 2014c]).

The day after writing the paragraphs above a gift arrived from Christian Nold; a book describing his Bio Mapping and Emotional Map projects in which he charts people's excitement using a combination of GPS and a sensor like that of a lie detector. Starkly described, this rings all sorts of warning bells. It seems to be reproducing the invasive strategy of a hyper-accelerated information culture; indeed, when news of Nold's work first reached the mainstream media he was inundated with "estate agents in California wanting an insight into the geographical distribution of desire... advertising agencies wanting to emotionally re-brand whole cities" (Nold 2014, 4). But what Nold did then was to turn the work on its head; he shared his data with his participants and let them re-encode it with their own associations and stories. I think he is not exaggerating when he writes that "[T]alking about their body data in this way, they are generating a new type of knowledge combining 'objective' biometric data and geographical position, with the 'subjective story' as a new kind of psychogeography" (2014, 5).

While I am not sure exactly how (and feel I have no right to speculate), there is in the principles of the democratic yet esoteric dynamics of Nold's emotional mapping something that might be drawn upon to produce multiple means of inviting people to address the city's "body data" through their own subjective encodings and then share them; complementary actions to the 'situational *dérive*', an 'art of memory' re-encoding of the city's surface and ambulatory architecture's soft redevelopments, a fourth step towards a 'new kind of psychogeography' for the 'new psychogeographers'.

The fifth step might be to find ways of keeping the encodings hidden from the techno-linguistic automatisms of state and commerce; defiantly uneven, baroque and hard to read narratives and associations conjured by active subjectivities make for maps that are time-consuming for commercial or informational interpretation to make usable sense of. This is an example of slow revolution; not a sudden rupture which leaves everything still to be done and everyone vulnerable to power in other masks, but longstanding in both prosecution and effects: "we need to slow down and be more aware and reflexive in order to be able to adapt when events change rapidly. The starting point is refusal. The direction is made by walking. An end-point is avoided... [T]he trick is to identify tendencies in the present which suggest alternative paths out of current crises" (Chatterton 2012, 165, 169).

The old argument against a slow revolution was that the working class was incapable of sustaining 'enemy within' institutions that could produce their own new ideology, such as university colleges once could for a nascent capitalism. Now EVERYONE is struggling to sustain institutions that produce anything much more than their own reproduction; content is progressively draining away in favour of a neo-liberal phantasmagoria of 'value for money', customer satisfaction, 'enterprise' and league tables. Space is in flow; where very recently it became suddenly clear that no one in the global economy has a job for life, so now it is even clearer that no one has a life for life. It is in the spaces of those "no ones", in the darknesses and precious nothingnesses of subjectivities, that we must form our invisible committees and invisible colleges.

The work of slow revolutionaries is to place a nail in the flow, to subject it to the torque of resistance, upset and the foot stuck out to trip, to everywhere block and barricade revolutionary capitalism, refusing to "wipe the slate clean" but instead to conserve and détourn the smears on the slate (this is why we love the everyday and its ruins) against the imperative to "start again from scratch", conserving and transforming obstacles and burdens into mini-barricades, chicanes and blockades. In her Performance, Transport and Mobility (2014) (in which I am 'outed' as something of an anti-modernist romantic), Fiona Wilkie rightly associates "the advocacy of slow travel... with slow food, signal[ling] 'a concern for locality, ecology and quality of life'" (36); that is not where our interest in walking's slowness should most lie, but rather in what it gives to walking in fluidity and resistance "against both the speed and the passivity of contemporary life" (37).

We are working in the aftermath of the Arab Spring and, to a lesser extent, Occupy, when for a while just by walking into a place and then holding onto it could bring down Power. Everywhere that affordance has been rolled back by states and freelance reactionaries, but that should tell us that, in turn, the reaction can itself be rolled back; that in a slow revolution sudden breaks are only ever the opening and that reaction is only ever a shifting of the grounds we can quietly retake.

Given the threat to subjectivity in an "age of infinite acceleration of the infosphere" when "boundless enhancement of disembodied imagination leads to... flight from one object to another" (Berardi 2012, 10, 116), rather than producing a new carnival of architectural or geographical expressivity, contemporary psychogeography may do better to draw upon the dematerialisations of the art object, the co-option of everyday processes (like mapping) and anachronisms like slow analogical coding, performance and iconoclastic practice (while rejecting its iconoclastic principles) as the collective means to discreetly navigate a creative space between a hiddenness within subjectivities' interior worlds and invisible encodings upon an unremovable and uncensorable everyday.

I have wandered from the edge of a supermassive black hole to the strategic terrain of a "new kind of psychogeography"; things are looking brighter...

Uh-oh!

8: gros and romanticism

Frédéric Gros's book *A Philosophy of Walking* was published in English translation in 2014 by the leftist publishing house Verso (having sold over 40,000 copies in French). At the Bristol (UK) Festival of Ideas he gave a talk on it, which I attended. I had read his book. It follows Rebecca Solnit's *Wanderlust* (2000), which in its turn had followed Morris Marples's *Shanks's Pony* (1960), in rooting modern non-functional walking in the nineteenth-century romantic movement and in privileging literary practice. At variance with Solnit, however, Gros, in both book and talk, excluded women from the narrative. When challenged during the Q&A he was embarrassed and ineffectually contrite; he said he had realised to his horror what he had done after the book had gone to press, and yet he did nothing to rectify his exclusions either in the translation or in his talk.

Gros attempts to relocate radical walking to an actively anti-modernist tendency, championing a direct, uncluttered and innocent encounter with the terrain; aligning it with a romanticism mostly stripped of 'terror sublime'. He describes his walks as always beginning with a break from the performance of his everyday life, putting aside technology, domesticity, work and the city, breaking from sociability, in order to follow in the footsteps of a romantic walking that once confidently testified "to presence and mystical fusion" (2014, 181).

Nothing new in any of that, of course, though it is perhaps surprising that a restatement of some very old ideas generally available elsewhere could garner quite such an audience. Perhaps the dynamic of his success was revealed during the Q&A session, when in what he described as "the great question of walking", Gros made it clear that he saw himself in the progressive camp, a fellow-traveller alongside situationists, and against conservatism.

Why did this bother me so much? On the train home, I repeatedly rehearsed to myself a critique of Gros's nostalgia for the authentic and the pre-modern. Each time it sounded a little more like the accusations levelled against psychogeographers, both occult and politically revolutionary: that, despite their roots in the modernist disruptions and fragmentations of neo-Dadaist and situationist iconoclasm, they all share a sense of loss of authenticity, a nostalgia for a sense of a presence that was more accessible in pre-modern eras, a preference for the antiquarian over the modern, and a savouring of physical and biological ruin and social redundancy over the revolutionary contradictions of production and social organisation.

If Gros's narrative stood up to scrutiny (and I was struggling to land many blows), it would mean that the two main traditions of resistant ambulation – the romantic tradition that began with radical literary walkers (most lively now in ecologically informed visual art, 'new nature writing', performance and poetry) and the disruptive and iconoclastic Dada deambulations and situationist *dérives* – had disappeared into each other. Gros co-opted Baudelaire, Benjamin, surrealism and situationist ambulations (2014, 180) into a narrative of "subversive" (177) urban strolling only different to romantic pedestrianism in the degree of its immersion in the Real: "[T]he great romantic walker... is fulfilled in an abyss of fusion, the stroller in a firework-like explosion of successive flashes" (181).

On my return from the talk I began to read avidly, almost desperately. I soon found that it was not only Gros, but writers such as Alastair Bonnett (2009), Jacques Rancière (2009, 6-7) and Sam Cooper (2013) who identified the *dérive* as romantic. Their interpretations struck deep into a practice I had always regarded as disruptive, anti-essentialist, anti-realist and subversive. The more I read, the more fuzzy seemed the break from romanticism on which I had tried, following others, to found my own wobbly walking; at the very least, with legs astride, trying to walk on both sides of the abyss. But Gros, Bonnett, Rancière and Cooper seemed to deny that abyss in favour of shades of Thomas Gray.

Gros, a handsome and, in manner, modest speaker, had made a hugely ambitious play: his argument is that all walks (including many far removed from admiring daffodils; dirty walks, humiliating walks, raging walks) are romanticist variations, greater or lesser fusions with what is already there. The revolutionary walk is not the making of the terrain itself, but simply a less successful fusion with it. Gros was close to bringing the entire context of the pedestrian arts to stasis – "when you are walking, nothing moves" (37) – forcing us to ask a question most of us probably thought we had resolved long ago: what is it that the situationist-inspired, performance and post-art influenced *dérive* does that distinguishes it from a romantic walking with a radical veneer?

9: yes to romanticism and beyond

To walk as an exchange of presences, not to walk beyond the human, not yet, but to walk alongside ideals and things as companions, to walk sociably, footsteps stretching out the hours, living longer but not forever, slowing light and bending time, but possessing neither. Any new landscape we may discover is inside ourselves, not a possession, but a gratitude for the exchange of presences with the landscape within us and our attending to and tending the terrain without (Kloetzel & Pavlik 2010, 7). Understanding that there is no external and objective "landscape"; just as there is no modern world without foundations resting on the graves of the colonialised, some barely dug.

Some of what passes for "presence and mystical fusion" is a potent concoction of self-delusion, appropriation of the agency of others and the brutal excisions of a kind of historiographical cutting room floor; Richard Long believing he is walking in prehistory through Dartmoor, apparently oblivious to ancient deforestation and the remnants of industry, Philip Marsden claiming a 10,000 year old burial site as a product of "the same awe we still feel at the dramatic features of the land" (2014, 11) or Robert Macfarlane for whom it is "instantly obvious why prehistoric people had chosen to bury their dead in such a location" (2012, 50).

One of the problems with Macfarlane's much read *The Old Ways*, with its titular hint, is that while it encompasses all sorts of experiences, pranks, risks and thought experiments, somehow it never allows its variegation to fully infect its traditionalism. It will not set its whole project at the mercy of the road. *The Old Ways* repeats the pattern of Linda Cracknell's *Doubling Back* and Simon Armitage's *Walking Home*: beginning with the dropping of dignities (Cracknell in drainage ditches, Macfarlane trespassing on a snow-covered golf course, Armitage in tangents off the Pennine Way) for adventures in thinking and feeling, only to return to a reinvigorated lack of ambition (though no lack of bravery or stamina or good companions), a confirmation that having glanced down the side alley and at the ABC (anomalous black cat) of Fortean things, having crawled in the back garden, it is still the 'main road' (even when that is constituted by a mountain pass), conserved by its perilous narratives, picturesqueness and vulnerability to gaze and imagination, that is somehow more certainly real.

Starting in the excitement of the margins, dallying in childhood and absurdity, these books offer a frisson to tired arteries, a sharp smack on the bottom of romanticism, before settling back, braced now, into a walking that does not so much take up its bed as its mental armchair. Cracknell and Macfarlane both have a predilection for interpreting the journey; when that happens the mobility solidifies into a commodity that is reassuringly unique and recognisable.

While the 'new nature writing' may pose some threat to radical walking (more than that from the literary psychogeographers; for while there is very little room at the top of the literary greasy pole anyone can convince themselves that they 'appreciate' the natural world) it need have no fears of any new strand of neo-romanticism (very different from its own neo-romantic roots in, say, Arthur Machen, Hope Mirrlees or Paul Nash). In the business of intensity of experience, authenticity, the 'real', risk or immersion, radical walking need not shuffle back, embarrassed. It is on the other side of these writers, it does not have them in its sights, not because they are so far down the road, but because they are at its coat tails. I was struck very much by Jess Allen apologising for quoting Robert Macfarlane on a recent Walking Artists Network walk; we can unapologetically reference what Macfarlane and others have to offer and leapfrog over them. For Macfarlane's *The Old Ways* may begin in the everyday, rankle at CCTV, take a swipe at Long ("a tiger pacing in a cage"[17]), contemplate "walking as séance" (21), embrace Nash, Powell & Pressburger and Nan Shepherd, but it soon joins itself to the front of that procession of canonised literary walkers that stretches back through Gros and Solnit to Marples; its brief *dérive* followed by epic trails with fixed destinations.

Radical walking tops all this by its clinging to the rim of the abyss not as an extreme moment on a mountain pass but as the *modus vivendi* of precarity that mythogeography promotes and that Clive Austin devotes a full-length movie, *The Great Walk* (2013), to championing: the walk of uncertainty in "uncertain times" done anywhere. Macfarlane does not have the resources to maintain his instability away from epic terrains, despite moments when he does 'throw' himself – collecting "seeds, dust, leaf fragments" in the resin on his bare feet, or getting lost seeking the landscape of rocks recomposed by Manus MacLennan. Though he has written elsewhere about the situationists, when, in *The Old Ways*, he searches for an equivalent to the Palestinian *sarha* he seems unaware of either *dérive* or going *a zonzo*.

We need not be cowed by authenticity, nor from admiring these writers for their attention to detail. But we can bring something from post-dramatic performance that goes beyond their romanticist authentic and that is the facility to stage authenticity; when the mask fits it disappears. Knowing that masks are authentic things made of vital matter, which express as well as hide. And from a modernist art tainted by theatre we can draw from Yves Klein, who put his signature on the sky; we can appropriate his absurdly inflationary gesture for an effective asymmetrical relation to climate change, a more appropriate relation to the environment we partly constitute, applying satellite capture techniques to the global climate's accelerationism, aware that our harmonies may not be the same as other parts of 'nature', that a good parasite does not kill its host, that sustainability will only come with excess, at the moment we grasp our monstrosity, that our uncanniness is a product of 'Nature'; and that a 'new psychogeography' honed to finding wonders in alleyways will be better placed than ecologists, who are too busy naturalising globalisation, when it comes to turning the oil tanker.

What the new romanticism lacks is unreal risks; the walking that mostly informs it, while its efforts and dangers are real and its paths exceptional, is hardly unpredictable. It has yet to "step outside the human bubble", in the words of the Dark Mountain manifesto. Again, radical walking can be, already is (if it would only acknowledge it itself) beyond these new romantics; the epic trails taken by Gros, Cracknell and Macfarlane (and farcically failed by Armitage [2012]) are safely separated by their own estrangement, their depredation is part of a complicated movement within which distinctions between wild and human-built environment are increasingly disappearing, boundaries between city and countryside eroded materially and mentally (I, now, no longer get asked repeatedly "can you drift in the countryside as well?"), and public and private meshing ("[M]aybe there is neither public nor private space any more... the boundary between physical space and the sphere of pure information has been blurred" (Nawratek 2012, 21). Against, and complementary to, the spread of aggressive 'liberalising' markets there is a generation-long Thatcherite riptide of anti-social appropriations and privatisations of public space "rel[ying] on a profoundly reactionary belief that human beings, like certain animal species, have an inbuilt 'territorial instinct' and will only defend their own territory" (Wilson 1991, 153). Radical walkers do not need to go lining up with the siege defenders of public space or wilderness, nor enter into exciting hypervelocity-embraces with globalised information space; instead we can seek out and define our own holey spaces. Rather than bemoaning "zones that are no longer really either town or countryside" (Wilson 1991, 9) we can enjoy the edgelanding of everywhere. Buddleia, anonymous animal migrations and expanding microbial colonies are our allies in the marinated terrains of climate change, and we can help them by opening up disruptive 'wild channels' across our cities and wondering if *Wolfen* (1981, director: Michael Wadleigh) is a documentary from the future.

In her *Doubling Back*, Linda Cracknell writes a wonderful chapter on her formative childhood explorations of her back garden. Unlike Cracknell's back garden where she was "secure between its taut wires fences" (2014, 13), as a child I lived in a road of new suburban semi-detached houses mostly occupied by couples with young children; as we grew up the wire fences rusted and fell down so that trails opened up across multiple gardens, offering us imaginary, social and, later, sexual playgrounds where a couple of rows of loganberries passed for a wilderness, a pear tree for a forest, a Himalayan Balsam for a Triffid, a coal bunker for a confessional, a shed for a pyramid to be grave-robbed and a blocked outdoor toilet for a bottomless pit of abjection.

What I learned from our inter-garden wanderings was that you do not have to trample, nor build ramparts in defence of the 'natural' or the old, but find a holey space as much in the everyday as in the exceptional, a place between the banal and the fanciful. That within private space there are gaps that are explorable and trespassable, connective and ambiguous; these are the efficacious spaces of subjective and intimate mutual exploration that Savile and his ilk appropriated for Power and that we must take back wherever they are taken from us. Today, there are new sets of abject 'arcades' in the gaps between fragments of modernism and malls defended from their nearest customers (Morrison 2012, 234-5), between shards of the 'fascist City Beautiful', in gaps in a city that, having "threatened and fractured human subjectivity" (Wilson 1991, 99) has done the same thing to itself.

And you have to like it. As Elizabeth Wilson once wrote, "we will never solve the problems of cities unless we *like* the urban-ness of urban life" (1991, 158). Yet, too often what has passed for radical criticism has been more of a dislike of the urban or the modern, a return to a reactionary strand of 'Merrie England' socialism that Alastair Bonnett has identified at work in occult-inflected anglo-psychogeography (2009). Too often the 'solutions' have been ascetic; smacking of the attitude of hikers who seem to know that what they are doing is "good for them", most fun when it is over (Gros's memories of the walk as better than the real thing [as Orlando says of pornography in Derek Jarman's *Jubilee*]).

At the end of *The Sphinx in the City* (1991), a book most often quoted for its characterisation of an oppressive male gaze and yet so full of optimism, Elizabeth Wilson writes something that reads rather oddly now: "Cities aren't villages; they aren't machines; they aren't works of art; and they aren't telecommunications stations. They are spaces for face to face contact of amazing variety and richness. They are spectacle – and what is wrong with that?" (158) Wilson prefaced these conclusions by describing how cities had offered the heroines of novels by Virginia Woolf and Miriam Henderson "not only adventure, but reassurance... its vast amorphousness maternal" (158) and by characterising her own part of London as "a disguise, a refuge, an adventure, a home" (159). If we take these multiplicitous urban virtues and set them to work against what is wrong with a hypermodern city then perhaps we can presume to re-write Wilson now: cities do not have to be spectacles; they could be villages, machines, works of art, telecommunications stations and spaces with the stillness necessary for face to face meetings and the instability conducive to fictional and multi-located contacts – and what would be so very wrong with that?

So, I have, and without apology, arrived among the problems and opportunities of the city from 'new nature writing'. For the city is a product of nature, both 'city' and 'nature' parts of a pattern of interlocking extended organisms and cold rhythms ('the maths is out there'). Or do human consciousness, planning and production (according to the romanticism that the 'new nature writing' is re-saying) operate on remote Platonic planes? Planes that conveniently allow the alternate idealisation of one and demonisation of the other: switching back and forth between 'innocent nature'/'corrupt society' and 'nature red in tooth and claw'/'welfare state'.

If we collapse those orders of binaries, we get to see how deep and interleaved the contradictions go: "the molten core.... producing an insulated reservoir of primal exogeneous (sic) trauma, the geocosmic motor of terrestrial transmutation... It's all there: anorganic memory, plutonic looping of external collisions into interior content, impersonal trauma as drive-mechanism"

(Land 2011, 498). We also get to see how possible, or at least potential, the resolutions are.

Through the voice of D. C. Barker, a fictional US professor involved in the search for alien intelligence, Nick Land uses a sci-fi/paranoia-thriller narrative trope, of the academic who stumbles upon a secret agenda (authorities seeking new patterns of social organisation and control under the guise of analysing patterns of intelligence), to propose a theoretical and strategic positioning for praxis; praxis being the "get a room!" where critical theory and action meet. As he writes, in Barker's flamboyant and wilfully obscure vocabulary (it's that same hallucinatory testing as the LPA subjected us to in *The Great Configuration*), he draws from numerous fields to map a terrain on which human agency is never 'above' anything, or across which nothing so unspontaneous and non-potent as "nature" could possibly dominate, but then at the final moment... well, you'll see.

> "strip-out all the sedimented redundancy from the side of the investigation itself – the assumption of inten-tionality, subjectivity, interpretability, structure, etc. – what remains are assemblies of functionally inter-connected microstimulus, or tic-systems: coincidental information deposits, seismo-cryptions, suborganic quasireplicators (bacterial circuitries, polypoid diag-onalizations, interphase R-Virus, Echo-DNA, ionizing nanopopulations), plus the macromachineries of their suppression, or depotentation. Prevailing signaletics and information-science are both insufficiently abstract and over-theoretical in this regard. They cannot see the machine for the apparatus, or the singularity for the model..."

Struggling yet? I think we're supposed to be. Those hybrid terms are neologisms of Land/Barker's, they almost make sense, and on that 'almost' is where Land wants us to be thinking. Otherwise, the argument is fairly straightforward. He is asking: 'if we cut out all those excuses about circumstances, points of view and contexts, what are we really responsible for in this process we call "living"?' Most philosophies or critical discourses, he proposes, cannot help us with that question because they are too busy talking to themselves about their own language or wasting their energy leaping over life and straight into theory. But if a way of being could be both tangled up in things *and* be those things themselves...

> "...an approach that is cosmic-abstract – hyper-materialist – and also participative, methods that do not interpret assemblies as concretizations of prior theories..."

OK, now this is becoming inspiring. And maybe you are recognising some references to this that I have made earlier in this book, remembering vaguely the contexts? Land/Barker is promising to tell us the way to jumble together the universe as a single entity, as a layer of ideal shapes and figures, as the immediate bruising reality of all the things bumping around us, and then add our agency to it in such a way that we can produce something the like of which has not been even imagined let alone seen before... how is he/he (ha ha!) going to do it? By being:

> "entirely intractable to subject/object segregation, or to rigid disciplinary typologies. There is no order of nature, no epistemology or scientific metaposition, and no unique level of intelligence. To advance to this area, which is the cosmos, requires..."

What can it be? He's just pulled down all the skylines of romanticist illusion and academic self-interest! No longer will we be subjected to disciplinary blinkers posing as theories of knowledge. In their place... what revelation?

> "...new cultures or – what amounts to the same things – new machines." (Land 2011, 495)

Well, that was disappointing. It all looped back on itself. He/He (ho ho!) got rid of all the humanist hubris about Nature and Autonomy for us, prepared the ground for our participation, mapped some of the patterns along which we might slide, but when it came to providing the... ahah!!! Maybe that's the point, we're just left with our own loneliness and a load of tired "machines" (I know he doesn't mean internal combustion engines, I know he means a flow and a break in the flow connected to all the other flows, and a break connected to all the other breaks, but he/he (he he!) might as well be talking about an Audi) and so when we finally get to the uplifting moralising I was going to write for the end of this section, about how nobody and nothing is going to make anything new for us, but we (and the cosmos) will have to do it for ourselves, then you will realise that, along with all the other romanticist and neo-romanticist longers for fusion, it is best, for now, if I wait in slowness and quietness, for a moment to come when nature and agency are superseded by something no one will or ever could predict.

10: psychogeography never existed

In the summer of 2014 I chanced upon Alistair Bonnett's latest book in the window of an independent bookshop in a small Dorset town. It was the first I knew of *Off The Map* (2014). Mindful that we were to be fellow-contributors to a book of essays on contemporary psychogeography in the UK (Richardson, forthcoming), I snapped it up and read it the next day. I knew Bonnett had written extensively on the role of nostalgia in psychogeography, I had seen him give the keynote address to the *TRIP: Territories Re-Imagined: International Perspectives* conference in Manchester in 2008, and the biographic note on the dustcover of *Off the Map* described him as "[F]rom 1994-2000... editor of the avant-garde, psychogeographical magazine *Transgressions: A Journal of Urban Exploration*".

Off the Map was not the book I was expecting. It describes quirky and anomalous places, mostly researched online, more in the manner of a *Sunday Times* feature writer than an academic or a radical activist. Characterised in an online *Guardian* review as "a work of armchair geography... an implicit critique of traditional boots-on-the-ground psychogeography" (Gallagher 2014, 7), it is not unlike Paul Farley and Michael Symmons Roberts' *Edgelands* where the poets' enthusiasm for landscape description outruns their experiential evidence. Even where Bonnett has made visits to the places he describes they are rather cursory ones: a daytime expedition to a deserted dogging site yields one descriptive sentence, his clamber onto a traffic island is briefer still: "as soon as I'm... on to the island I feel acutely self-conscious... After five minutes I'm safely back on the mainland" (Bonnett 2014, 114).

More surprising, though, is how Bonnett uses his Introduction to *Off the Map* to renounce nomadic thinking, psychogeography and spatial theory. To illustrate how wrong he had been all along he describes the *dérives* of Psychogeography Associations and Societies in which he had participated in the 1990s. According to Bonnett they consisted of only two tactics: the intuitive pursuit of occult energy and "purposely getting lost by using a map of one place to navigate oneself around another" [2014, 5]). The walks had been "little more than pegs on which to hang our interpretative essays, which usually came with pendulous bibliographies" and were "very tame" compared to place hacking (52).

Even when taking into account the tendency to exaggerate such self-deprecations, there is a serious implication here. Bonnett's account suggests that there has *never* been a practice in the UK worthy of being called psychogeographic (other than perhaps as a literary practice). Rather than providing some rebalancing of romantic and situationist walkings or reconciling the varieties of psychogeography with different theoretical currents (I still remember Anna Powell's musings on the possibilities of a Debord/Deleuze crossover), *Off the Map* proposes that a practical psychogeography never actually existed in the UK.

In the very early 2000s, when I first got excited about walking as a resistant and disruptive practice, I had checked out online the, then still mostly active, Psychogeography Associations and Societies in the UK and North America. I found their postings and publications acerbic, sectarian, illuminating, bombastic and sometimes engagingly occult, but I had never supposed that they were, in practice, imaginary. I had regarded them as mostly honest attempts on which others might build. Now, though, I was beginning to feel that they might be black holes of anti-practice.

11: old stuff

Without the International Lettrists and Situationist International (IL/SI), their radical 'liking' for the city, their revolutionary desire to realise it fully, free of capital, and their tactics for getting there (*dérive*, *détournement* and psychogeography) we might now be far more vulnerable than we are to purveyors of novelty tours and self-deluding 'leisure walking plus', to Deborah Knowles's advocacy for "techniques of psychogeography... advantageously employed in business and management research" [Knowles 2009, 47], to the commercialisation of Joshua Berlow's plans to "buy real estate, get a headquarters... charge money for *dérives*" [quoted in Glover, 2014, unpaginated]) to Walk 21 (motto: "leading the walking movement") and other hegemonising operations.

While not all radical walkers or walking artists admire or borrow from the IL/SI, most of them have heard of and have opinions about *dérives*, psychogeography, *détournement* and constructing situations (though sometimes the terminology varies). Over the years I have met a few walkers who have set their face uncompromisingly against the legacy of the IL/SI, but there have been many more who, by careful study or casual absorption, have deployed and transformed situationist techniques to their own ends.

Despite this legacy, debt perhaps, Alastair Bonnett's contemptuous characterisations of *dérive* and psychogeography are not exceptional, just the most recent in a long list of comparable assessments from surprising sources: former-situationist Ralph Rumney (the *dérive* is a pub crawl), Rebecca Solnit (it's all just *flânerie*), Doreen Massey (laddish pranks), Simon Sadler ("a sort of therapy" that never garnered any real data [1998,

80]), Geoff Nicholson (pretentious tricksiness [2008, 144-6, 149-64]), a pre-renunciation Bonnett ("blokish left-bank bar-crawl[s]... White anarchists barg[ing] their way through multicultural Paris" [1996, 24]), early Merlin Coverley (same as Solnit) and the Materialist Psychogeographic Affiliation's Steve Hanson: "a tradition in the sense of, say, Morris Dancing" (2007, 11).

These denigrations hit right at the workings of what, for many walkers, have been *essential motors* for interrogating and provoking idealist walking into interesting hybrids; they reach right to the door of IL/SI. If the motors have always been useless, then psychogeography's history is phantom and any connection between contemporary *dérivistes* and a tradition of useful precedents is fanciful. Are the streets being pulled from beneath our feet? If Bonnett's assertions are right, they would confirm Bradley L. Garrett's impression that the geographers driving the 1990s' revival of psychogeography "write about it without ever practising it" and his assertion that Bonnett's own *Transgressions: A Journal of Urban Exploration* had been "snuffed out... by academia's... failure to ground theory *in* practice" (2009, unpaginated).

I acquired and read the first four of the five issues of *Transgressions*. Online I found and read parts of the fifth. Across all four complete issues that I read, only two theoretical articles made reference to any findings from an actual walk. The reports of 'drifts' in *Transgressions* were as pinched as their characterisations in *Off The Map* (or more so, as the occult, appropriately perhaps, seems not to have materialised). One report describes the wrong map tactic used to little effect, another (by The Urban Research Group, 1998) consists of a long gloss about imperialism and a description of cursory visits to Next, the National Trust of Scotland and a student bar (most tourists display greater agency and marginality) while an encounter with a veteran is uncomfortably reminiscent of the post-colonialist human-botanising of Geoffrey Murray's "Natural History of the Streets" (1939, 305). A scribe for a day-long drift on local trains complains of "seeing very little" (Boyle, 89); two short articles do identify 'green worlds' on traffic islands, with one ending bathetically as its solo *dériviste* is chased into a church by a car owner. The 1996 double issue has only one account, a solo walk made while knitting a map; it begins promisingly, but lapses into functionality ("I am here because it's windy... I'm a bit bored... I need some food... I am tired" [MacRae 1996, 12]). Taken together, these reports confirmed Bonnett's description and echoed Brad Garrett's suspicions; as far as it is recorded in *Transgressions*, the dismissive comments of Rumney, Solnit and others reflects the reality of 1990s' psychogeographical practice.

Remarkably, given such mind-numbing accounts, some folk were still willing to subject themselves to such parodies of the *dérive* even after the Psychogeographic Associations had faded from the scene; Steve Hanson describes a dour algorithmic walk in Greenwich in 2004: "the walk's passengers were lab rats, stuck on a wheel... adherents to the instrumental rationality of some nuthouse exercise yard" (2004, 7). I am mindful that these 'drifts' are hostage to their reporting, but I also remember being on the wrong end of this 'drifting' at the 2008 *TRIP* conference; first a tedious, functionalist 'wrong map' exercise (it's a 'catapult', not an end in itself!), then an all-male group marching (without exploration) from site to site of historic interest (sites of former plague pits were particularly popular). In what I have long felt to be a telling moment, we encountered a woman liberally applying fake tan to her legs as she perched on the steps of a bridge. The group strode on without remark, oblivious or uninterested; it was more like a history class than a meander of dispersed eroticism.

Just in case that experience was not evidence enough, I sought out other 1990s' psychogeographical newsletters, online and in Stewart Home's *Mind Invaders* (1997); mostly not as bleak as the reports from *Transgressions*, still, when all taken together, my reading demonstrated that the activists of the 1990s' Psychogeography Associations and Societies were attempting to 'drift' with very little access to toolkits of tactics or useful precedents, almost wholly dependent on glosses upon Guy Debord's *The Theory of the Dérive* and a spatial taxonomy limited to sites of "entry into or exit from certain zones" (Debord 1981c, 62). That their routinised and simplistic approach was still being slavishly reproduced in 2004 or 2008 (perhaps somewhere even now) is testimony to the morbid and annihilating energy of ideas floating about on an absence of complex practice.

This is not a fun opportunity for laughing at ineffective lefties doing their best in hostile circumstances. This is a dangerous situation for radical walking: to have, as even part of its inheritance, a vampire tradition of wishful thinking founded on the exhumations of a few dry, fleshless tactics. How is that going to stand up to a revival of romantic walking with its resources of poetry, escapism, heritage and deep ecological sensitivity in the face of global climate derangement?

Photo: Glen Stoker

12: wooooooohooooo!!!!

It was the much maligned literary and occult psycho-geographers who came to my rescue back in the early 2000s. It was they who most vividly maintained, if sometimes in uncomfortably obscurantist, clubable and misogynistic ways, a space for the irrational, unconscious, haptic, poetic and noumenal. It was they who identified where inner life imbeds itself in architectural form, who knew how to walk and explore and to identify where the psychogeographical becomes mythogeographical and engage directly with ideology in motion: "the horny Victorian parson building his hilltop church and the 21st Century racist ruling his internet micronation from a Hackney tower-block... the arc of London's landmarks, as seen from the marshes... a series of ideologies exposed through architecture" (Rees 2013, 129).

In a secularised society, with strongly empiricist academic traditions, it has been fairly easy for leftist critics to nail occult psychogeography to the same milieus as New Age mysticism and English Heritage: "No occultism, John Dee or spectres. No hermeticism", demanded the Materialist Psychogeographic Affiliation (Hanson 2007, unpaginated). And there are, for sure, plenty of examples of wilful obfuscation, sentimentality, sexism and obtuse nationalism on the parts of occult psychogeographers; but there has also been a patrician insensitivity and misunderstanding on the part of leftist critics about the dynamic contradictions and material embeddings of occult psychogeography: where these "have a conservative, traditionalist sound to them (and, of course, they do), it is partly because so many socialists and communists remain unable to imagine social liberation as something that grows from within an existing society rather than as something imposed by a modernist elite" (Dusty Bin, 2009, 63).

One of those 'socialists and communists' was a pre-renunciation Alastair Bonnett who portrayed occult psychogeography as driving radicalism into an embrace with nostalgia and the left-reactionary tradition of 'Merrie England' to the detriment of historic authenticities. Reading his key paper on the subject, I sensed a mis-match between the adroitness of his critique and the evidence about its target; Bonnett characterises the predominating attitude of Manchester Area Psychogeographic's activists on a visit to a derelict graveyard as "preservationism" (2009, 64). Yet their account, quoted at length by Bonnett, suggests other priorities: "[F]from the vandalised vaults to the used condoms, the overgrown lawns and trees, the graffiti, the remnants of the Church and the weathered gargoyles, the atmosphere and emotional responses generated were absolutely overwhelming. And to think Aldi are going to destroy it and turn it into a buck cheap supermarket" (MAP 1996, 4).

Why is this "preservationism"? It mentions old, eroded and damaged architecture, but mostly it describes embodied encounters with texture, with abjection and ambience, and the equalisation of remnants of church and sex. If it seeks to "preserve" anything it is the transforming and depredating rot and decay; something to throw in the face of an "antiquarian walk... [that] breathes life into the dead, restores, by the power of... imagination, a splendour that has departed, and where the mighty have been overthrown, raises them again to their seats" (Murray, 1939, 78). MAP's walk *resists* that kind of heritage "preservationism", a kind complemented in its homogenisation to ideology by Aldi's wholesale destruction. Two sides of the same coin: one destroying the fabric, the other its radical meaning. It is clearly the radical meaning that MAP seeks to preserve; its means, an embodied immersion in rot, abjection and used condoms.

I have enjoyed and learned a great deal from works by occult psychogeographers. Iain Sinclair's *Lights Out For The Territory* was important in getting me exploring and sensitising me to complexities, ironies, textures, narratives and layering. The neo-romantic influences of the literary psychogeographers (Arthur Machen's *The London Adventure* or Hope Mirrlees's *Lud-In-The-Mist*) have partially shaped my re-imagining of the terrains I explore; simple ways to write code over the top of an existing space and a semi-allegorical approach to the built environment with precedents in works like *Hypnerotomachia Poliphili* and in encoded architecture like that of pretty much any medieval English town with a protective church of St Michael in its northern part. I admired writers like the Fortean Jonathan Downes (who might well be surprised to find himself listed alongside works by occult psychogeographers) for books like *The Owlman & Others* which interweaves its author's personal psychic disruption with slippery narratives and a morphing landscape. Various literary homages to Pan were a useful way into the hyper-sensitisations of "pan-ic" and Kierkegaardian dread on the road. Even the defocusing of the eyes vouched for by the more convinced "to see fairies" could be turned into a useful exploratory tool.

Though I have been embarrassed by the antiquarianism and credulity of much of what has passed for occult psychogeography, what I realise now, in a flash of understanding that cuts through a grey mire of defeatist leftist interpretation, is that it was these very obfuscations of occultism and the well-worn tracks of the uncanny (in a virtuous ambiguity that is as objective as it is human) that brought at least some *dérivistes*, including myself, into an immersed rather than a token practice. That, whatever their faults, if judged on the basis of practical effects, and when compared to the dry materialist jaunts and licensed ennui of the 1990s described in Bonnett's *Transgressions* journals, it was occult psychogeography that kept the 'drift' alive and practised, and inspired the gothic Marxism and anti-ideological manoeuvres of the likes of Manchester Area Psychogeographic.

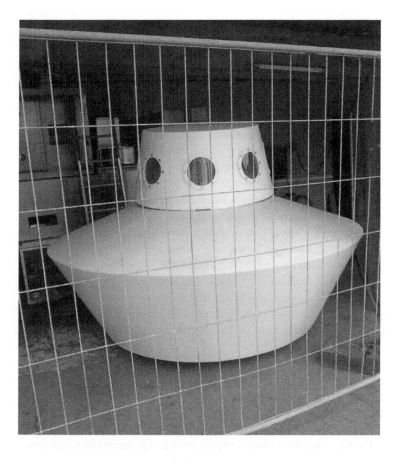

13: recently

In the first half of 2014 I went on a walk with Glen Stoker, exploring a small part of Stoke-on-Trent for a couple of hours. I later re-shaped our adventure into a walk for the city's Airspace Gallery that included eyes-shut dancing to Lou Reed ("these are the stories of Edgar Alan Poe, not exactly the boy next door") on the stage of the local theatre, standing in waste ground imagining movies on the no longer existing screen of a demolished cinema, group walking in the shape of a horse in response to a horseshoe-shaped doorway, using concrete steps as mental maps, slow motion walking around a Richard Long exhibition, striking matches between statues of a steel worker and the designer of the Spitfire, walking together masked, listening to messages from the fabric of a huge derelict chapel and then speaking them from its giant pulpit, shaking hands through railings, and using a portal to a Tesco supermarket and a benchmark in a side street wall as movement scores.

Things are very different now from the days when the Psychogeographical Associations (the first 'new psychogeographers') relied on thirty-year-old SI texts long divorced from practice. Today, there are numerous handbooks and accounts that can be sifted for tactics, complementing the assemblies of radical walkers and opportunities to engage with a wide range of ambulatory practices. Exemplary publications include

- Tim Brennan's numerous short books on his 'manoeuvres' (1999a, 1999b, 2002, 2011)
- Simon Pope's *London Walking: a handbook for survival* (2000)
- Mike Pearson and Michael Shanks's *Theatre/Archaeology* (2001)
- Stuart Horodner's *walk ways* (2002)

- Francesco Careri's *Walkscapes* (2002)
- Jim Colquhoun's *A Company of Vagabonds* pamphlets on walks to St Peter's Seminary, Lennox Castle Asylum and other sites (2003)
- the *Mis-Guides* to *Exeter* and *Anywhere* created by Wrights & Sites (2003, 2006)
- Anna Best's *Occasional Sights – a London guidebook of missed opportunities and things that aren't always there* (2003)
- Tim Edensor's *Industrial Ruins* (2005)
- Carl Lavery's *25 instructions for performance in cities* (2005)
- Townley & Bradby's *Sweep and Veer* (2005)
- Simon Whitehead's *Walking to Work* (2006) and *Lost In Ladywood* (2007)
- John Davies's *Walking the M62* (2007)
- Tamara Ashley & Simone Kenyon's *The Pennine Way: The Legs That Make Us* (2007)
- Michael Bracewell & Linder's *I Know Where I'm Going* (undated)
- the 'Place: the place of self' chapter in Dee Heddon's *Autobiography and Performance* (2008, 88-123)
- *Walking, Writing & Performance* (2009) edited by Roberta Mock
- The Geography Collective's *Mission: Explore* (2010)
- *Bypass Pilgrim* by Roy Bayfield (2010)
- Harriet Hawkins and Annie Lovejoy's *insites – a notebook* (undated)
- Tom Stone's *Where to? From what? A (non, un, mis)Guide for Escape(ism) and Distraction* (2011)
- my own handbooks (Smith 2010a, Crab Man 2012a, Crab Man & Signpost 2012, Smith 2014a)
- *Walking With Cthulhu* by David Haden (2011)
- *Manual for Marginal Places* by Emma Cocker, Sophie Mellor and Simon Poulter (2011)
- Nick Papadimitrou's *Scarp* (2012)
- Jess Allen's *tilting@windmills* (2012)
- Brandon LaBelle's *Handbook for the Itinerant* (2012)
- Bryan Sonderman's *Walking Games* (2012)
- Tina Richardson's *Concrete, Crows and Calluses* (2013)
- Simone Kenyon and Neil Callaghan's instruction cards for *Lincoln*

Dances 2013
- Karen O'Rourke's *Walking and Mapping* (2013)
- the chapter "'Three miles an hour': Pedestrian Travel" in Fiona Wilkie's *Performance, Transport and Mobility* (2014, 18-41)

...and so on. Not to mention all the urban-explo materials from the likes of the late Ninjalicious, Bradley L. Garrett's *Explore Everything!* (2013) and the luscious publications of Julia Solis.

Gatherings have included:
- the *Site/Sight – Source/Resource* symposium (Exeter, UK, 2004)
- the fringe of the *Walk 21* conferences (until the coup against its fringe at the Zurich 2005 conference, though there is word that it may be loosening up again)
- *InTRANSIT* walks and talks in Kensington and Chelsea (2007)
- *Roam: A Weekend of Walking* at Loughborough University (2008)
- the *Mythogeography, Writing and Site-Specific Performance* conference (Plymouth, UK, 2008)
- the Loiterers Resistance Movement's *Get Lost* festival (Manchester, 2008)
- *Living Landscapes* conference in Aberystwyth (2009)
- *Ambulation* exhibition at Plymouth Arts Centre (2010)
- the ongoing *Still Walking* festivals in Birmingham, UK organised by Ben Waddington
- *Sideways Walking Festival/Trage Wegen* (Belgium, 2012)
- *On Walking* conference (Sunderland, UK, 2013)
- *Walk On* exhibition (2013-4)
- *B-Tour* festivals in Berlin and Belgrade (2013-4)
- *The Walking Encyclopedia* exhibition at Airspace (Stoke-upon-Trent, UK, 2014)
- the forthcoming *Where to? Steps Towards the Future of Walking Arts* at Falmouth (2015)

...and so on. The New York *Psy-geo-conflux* festivals for a number of years provided a place of exchange for activists and artists.

Many of the publications and events cited above have also popularised useful practical precedents: Fluxus scores, Yoko Ono's *Map Pieces* (1964), Brian Eno's *Oblique Strategies* (1975), and so on.

Although Simone Hancox (2012, 60) cites Rancière – on looking as action, interpretation as transformation – to affirm the value of single tactics, in many, if not most, cases the tactics offered, in the publications and events cited above, have come in the form of collections, guides, handbooks or toolkits. Carl Lavery's "25 instructions" (Lavery 2005) almost constitutes a lifetime's score. By practising a range of tactics the walker can develop their walking as a discipline, skills deployed and hybridised independently, as part of a recognisable 'mystery' (in the sense of a skilled trade). Accumulations of multiple tactics can tip over into qualitative change; into an uneven, evolving and always, and necessarily, partly covert 'life score'; what this is all about.

There are numerous websites that set out to provide their visitors with multiple resources for their own walking-related practices, or are so steeped in practice that it is hard for the visitor to avoid picking them up:

- *Psychogeographic Review*: www.bit.ly/walk001
- Gareth Rees's *Psychogeography*: www.bit.ly/walk002
- Tina Richardson's *Particulations*: www.bit.ly/walk011
- my own *Mythogeography*: www.bit.ly/walk005
- *The Haunted Shoreline*: www.bit.ly/walk006
- *The Contemporary Art of Walking*: www.bit.ly/walk008
- *The Fife Psychogeographical Collective*: www.bit.ly/walk009
- *Global Performance Artworks*: www.bit.ly/walk003
- *Deveron Arts' Walking and...* www.bit.ly/walk010
- *Artours*: www.bit.ly/walk014
- *The Walk Exchange*: www.bit.ly/walk007
- *flanerie: labor für gedanken & gänge*: www.bit.ly/walk012
- *Monique Besten*: www.bit.ly/walk004
- *Walking and Art*: www.bit.ly/walk013

- *Hybrid Flâneur*: www.bit.ly/walk015
- and, to make the point, *Not Another Psychogeography Blog*: www.bit.ly/walk016.

As well as the sheer volume of hard copy and online publications, there has also been a significant change of tone in psychogeographically informed writing, a greater commitment to openness and accessibility. Compare, say, the prose of John Rogers, Gareth Rees (whose bibliography for *Marshland* [2013] sends his readers spilling out to new resources) or Tina Richardson to that of the obfuscations of the London Psychogeographical Association or the early Iain Sinclair. Equally, you will not catch Nick Papadimitriou allowing the encounter with the geographical to become swamped by literary form or crypto-politics. And while the heroic solo art walk of Long and Fulton, inaccessible to most people due to its epic proportions, continues to garner admiration among arts managers (and the public), more recent walking performances, even when they are as epic as Elspeth Owen's, Jess Allen's or Monique Besten's, also tend to be more sociable. The general trend is democratic, but not necessarily yet transformational.

As part of my 'research' for this essay I opened up three large boxes of radical walking 'ephemera' that I have accrued unsystematically over the past seven or eight years; artworks and documentations collected from others' walks and walking-based projects. Of the 120 items recovered from the boxes, 26 are maps either designed for use on walks or describing exemplary walks, 14 are sets of instructions for walks and 6 are guidebooks for walking specified routes in a non-conventional manner, 6 are audio cds to accompany walks, 3 are 'randomisers' to guide walkers by chance and one is a pair of cardboard spectacles for use on a walk. That almost half of all the objects are specifically intended to be used for further walks rather than as documentations or souvenirs points to the dispersive rather than commodified nature of much recent walking. Maps and anti-maps, walking sticks, pointers, tools, consumables, detectors, sensors, locational devices, conductors for non-rational perception, models, pamphlets, guides, films, paintings, taxonomies of space, pocket sculptures, constructs and covert installations are all now readily available from walking artists; not in themselves, even together, constitutive of a strategy for radical walking, but components of a toolkit that anyone might collect and deploy in the future as part of such a strategy.

Mark James's exhibition *The Itinerant Toolkit* (2008-2010) was such an assemblage, collecting together and exhibiting (Sunderland and Plymouth) radical walkers' toolkits. Ostensibly "a resource and commissioning tool to examine the ideas that surround journeying as an artistic practice", and a context for its curator to engage in a dialogue about such journeying, it also served, by its simple accumulation of things, as a crude marker of the extent of these productions, adaptations and adoptions. James posed a practical question as a starting point for his research: "how do you carry your itinerancy?" (2009) A rather simplistic nomadist question, it presents the possibility of a radical critique of property – what do you *need* to carry with you? What can you carry with you without commerce or exchange? – and of addressing climate change and other migrations; a reparative and depressive slow mobility by which to counter disaster capitalism's rapidly developing uproars and perpetually breaking news.

The Itinerant Toolkit's library-like qualities are more fully realised in *The Walking Library* of Dee Heddon and Misha Meyers (2012 - ongoing). This takes a qualitative leap from *The Itinerant Toolkit*, which, despite its title, was mostly displayed in stationary mode within galleries. *The Walking Library* not only is an assembling of the ideas and texts of walking, but it walks. *The Walking Library* lends, reads, invites, gathers together, recites, discusses and includes. It is like a low-tech and mobile version of H. G. Wells's 'World Brain' (1938) with multiple branches (wheelbarrows, backpacks), a basic, but changing canon and an interactive and democratic recital and renewal of the collection. It is more than functional and provocative, it is part of its own strategy.

We could, perhaps, benefit from the rolling out of such a 'World Brain' at a larger scale, an evangelism for a flaky and always changing canon of shared texts – starting, just say, with Laura Oldfield Ford's *Savage Messiah* (2011), Lucy Furlong's poem-map *Amniotic City* (2013), Nan Shepherd's *The Living Mountain* (1997), Monique Besten's blogs and Raja Shehadah's *Palestinian Walks* (2007)... A 'World Brain' could also conserve and disperse encodings for a world-wide art of memory.

From all the gatherings, publications and projects listed above (only a fraction of what has been going on and sharply restricted geographically) it should be clear that a wide range of tactics is now available to anyone willing to seriously engage with radical walking. The kinds of ideas available to walkers and the ways of thinking them have changed in the last generation; there is a far deeper immersion of psychogeographical thinking *in practice* and there is a widespread if approximate understanding of psychogeography among the majority of practising art walkers. A generation of walkers, aware of the *dérive* though not beholden to it, are breaking down the separation between pedestrian immersion and theoretical thinking. Many contemporary walking artists have moved partially into academic research (like Morag Rose of the Loiterers Resistance Movement whose research on feminist psychogeography may begin to correct a massive omission); these practitioner-researchers are setting theory at the mercy of ambulatory practice to an extent without precedent in the 1990s. Whereas many nascent psychogeographers at that time seemed to flinch at the prospect of devising a complex walking practice, now many longstanding ambulatory explorers and artists engage uninhibitedly with psychogeographical and other ideas, while the recent emergence of Practice as Research and the broader applications of ethnography and auto-ethnography means that the academy is partially moving to meet them (a legacy of 'drifting' evident in Steve Hanson's ethnographic study of Todmorden [2014] or Andrew Molloy's PhD film *Myths of Belfast* [2015]), with attendant threats and temptations.

A Plastic Journey (2012)

Monique Besten walked from Amsterdam to Utrecht (64 km.) in 4 days, collecting and carrying all the plastic she found on her way. The goal was 'The 8th Continent', a weekend-long project about plastic organised by the artist collective 'de Metaalkathedraal'. 'A Plastic Journey' was documented on video and Monique was nicknamed 'The Plastic Crusader'.

14: the movement

Since the 1990s the burgeoning multiplicity of new walkers has changed the terrain for radical walking. The growth in useful rather than bewildering publications and in opportunities to gather together seems to reflect the growth in the practices themselves; both in the deepening sophistication of ambulatory practices and in the crude numbers participating. Where the LPA once created a mostly fictional organisation as a launch pad for occult texts (which I appropriated for the conceit of my own *Mythogeography* [2010a]), many walking artists and ambulatory activists today behave *as if they were* members of a fictive, subterranean and discreet, if undisciplined, organisation; an unlimited and unrestraining meshwork of subjectivities. There is no such organisation, of course; nor is there much reason for one: which is perhaps why imagining one might be enjoyable.

The Walking Artists Network already provides walkers with a means to connect with each other and organises very occasional events (though it has no detailed theoretical or evident organisational agenda). There is no reason to suspect that the variegation and exponential increase in walking practices will come to a halt soon. But is there a dialectical process at work within the increase and diversification? What if it masks a normalcy within it? What if the growth in disparate practices, by its very mass, generates a sudden condensation of practice, a tightening of connections? Might the development of a co-operative and relational (rather than literary and individualistic) psychogeography actually constrain the dispersal and performance of a practice that can only come from the subjective, whose performance is always 'to the side' of itself? I have no idea, but I have my suspicions.

The undemanding and minimum programme of WAN has created the space for multiplicity to flourish, but will it always continue to do so? Is it time to 'move on' from the loose and generous associations typified by WAN to a more agitational and dispersive network? Something with a harder edge, more evangelical, more at war with the Spectacle, and on a dissident footing with WAN. To open up a war on two fronts, acknowledging that it can be OK, in alliance, to emphasise differences once common ground has been long established. Time for a WAN fringe or an open infiltration? Time to break from the minimum constructs and 'leisure walks plus' of WAN to something more difficult and divisive and more protective of the history and revolutionary impulse inherited from the likes of LI/SI? Or, better, something simply additive. To add to the talking/walking shop a clearing house for tactics and strategic information such as surveys of spatial taxonomies, mythogeographies of variously connected locales and banks of esoteric/political codes for use in an art of memory?

How would you organise without a plan, without a hierarchy? Is 'leaderless resistance' possible? But (unlike its fascist and fundamentalist versions) really without any leaders, even ones in the shadows?

What if we collectively invented our own versions of a fictional, non-existent, octopus-like organisation of walkers of which each of us would be leader, but no one would be follower. The organisation(s) would be a joke, an effective cover, but mostly would serve to structure our individual work, so that we can continue to work in the "as if" of responsibility and collectivity, while having none and being bound to nothing (see the Wrights & Sites model below). Of course, everyone would be free to invent their own fictional organisations, but with the proviso, inevitably, that at some obscure and secret level we would all be, 'spiritually', a part of that even more fictional and submarine organisation. The emptiness, the voids created by such fictions, would operate as a powerful nothingness, a necessary irrational and non-organic hidden-ness, energising the flowing actions of (non) members. Its rule books would include G. K. Chesterton's *The Man Who Was Thursday* and its society histories would include the semi-bogus genealogy of walking in Clive Austin's mockumentary movie *The Great Walk* (2013)

For actual, limited-scale collective work, there is the exemplary model of Wrights & Sites' *modus vivendi* which is both organised and porous (after all, the escape of mythogeography from that organisation is why I am able to write this book). Because the members of Wrights & Sites can never agree on anything in either detail or principle, we proceed in the following way: we choose very general areas of agreement around practices to work with, then, for a specific project we make a bare collective structure that we can agree on. This structure will consist of Happenings-like spatial and temporal compartments which, by mutual consent we allot to each other. Then each of us, within our allocated, personal compartments, is free to put or do whatever we want without interference from the others (in reality there's often a minor element of negotiation, but the dominant mode is independence). Once the compartments are full the project is complete. This is how the *Mis-guides* were written and how the manifestos were assembled. It is how our 4 Screens videos were made: each member received a camera, a set starting and finishing time, one or two other agreed rules, and then were free to choose where and what and how to film. The results were then placed together and run simultaneously on a quartered screen (Wrights & Sites 2013). Would it be possible and desirable to roll out that model as a means of organising in small or medium-sized, temporary groups?

By making each of ourselves an 'anywhere' (Wrights & Sites 2006, 110-1) we can each learn to be a stranger to ourselves, and to be better strangers to each other, facilitating a kind of holey organising; creating bare collective structures in order to provide compartments for free activity? Although Wrights & Sites is quite incapable of collectively subscribing to or evolving a political meta-narrative, if you have ever heard or read one of the group's manifestos (www.bit.ly/walk017) you will know that while each of the policies or tactics or demands on its own can be deployed or realised under the conditions of the present political economy, the totality cannot.

Despite, or perhaps because of, the present dearth of organisation there is among dissident walkers a surprising commonality of general purposes and principles, alongside a huge range of different styles, approaches and genres. Without the need for the theoretical consistency required by an Association or Society structure, we still intermittently manage to subject ourselves informally to critique and debate; it is not all back-slapping. In both my *Mythogeography* and *Tourists/Terrorists: useful ambiguities in a search for models* (both 2010) I got it wrong: I tried to suggest empty models for people to fill with themselves. Later (Smith, 2012), studying the supposedly most passive, manipulated and alienated of consumers – tourists – I grasped just how profound and witty was their agency, and that it was from that agency that everything radical can start. For that reason, among others, I take subjectivities more seriously than most (as does psychogeography), and myths even more positively (as does occult psychogeography); I see not only obfuscation, ideology, the script of neo-liberalism and the 'shadows of gods', but also their revolutionary negation by actions that we cannot predict and should not try to second guess, but must instead await and respond to slowly and anonymously; a movement that does not require leadership but the cultivation of 'without qualities', the "I would prefer not to" of the human strike and immersion in the "deep crime" of life in the crowd.

While the transformation of radical walking by women is well afoot, black and ethnic minority walkers are barely visible at all in radical walking in the UK, and – for these separations are inextricably linked – class division continues to put a moat between practice and theory. The hybrids that poke their noses down the corridors of academia and into art studios are often still re-narrated as "bewildering" if they dare to show their faces in everyday public space. Neo-Dadaists and post-situationists may call for an 'everyday creativity' to replace art, but the division of theory and practice is such, powered by contrasting relations to production, fracturing along a variety of stress lines, that it too often consigns such creativity to tiny parcels of content-based provocation, milieu specialisation and formal experimentation; niches unvisited by most people in their everyday lives. While the relation between practice and theory is being transformed in the academy by the return to actual practice (a rare anomaly of institutional content), there is at present no similar prospect for a resolution of practice and theory in everyday life.

A challenge for a new radical walking will be to extend "women's rights to the carnival, intensity and even the risks of the city" (Wilson, 1991, 10) to other presently excluded groups; a growth that will be the business of those who are growing without cultivation; of the creepers not head gardeners. In the tactics of radical walking we have the (limited) means to take back some of the surplus value drained from the most exploited people in the city: how then do we disperse those means to free pleasure in the city, getting them out beyond the artists and to those who are least well-prepared to recognise or disposed to use them? Radical walking must learn the creative means of absenting itself in order for others to walk radically; its mortal remains left behind as fallen strategies – global art of memory, collective independence, war on two fronts, open infiltration, leaping over neo-romanticism's head – for others to pick up or crush to dust as they walk far beyond.

15: the problem is walking itself

Walking since Richard Long and Hamish Fulton has sometimes been addressed as a branch of Land Art. This categorisation serves as a useful reminder that even the most transitory and lightly stepped passage rearranges the ground in footprints and bathes places in the photographic images 'taken' of/f them; such small interventions are ambulant architectures.

Easily fetishised in their individual parts, any collective description of such interventions is fraught with planning, urbanist and journalistic traps. The relentless squeezing of the possibilities for artists in public space has had the positive effect of their returning to that space, and along with other pedestrians, not as artists as much as lay architects; leaving the traces of their journeys rather than depositing product, changing images rather than completing representations, drawing *critically* on Robert Smithson's 'site/non-site' or Long's collecting mud and rocks for the gallery, taking these and other materials on destinationless wanders (on routes of relentless portals), refusing to be ruined (or being refused ruin) by arrival. The contradiction for power is that the more it denudes and disarms the public and the public artist, the more it clothes and weaponises the nomad.

Walking, by its transient nature and by its relations to materials, has always been placed problematically, paradoxically and productively in relation to 'site-specificity'; the 'site-specific' being that aesthetic approach which privileges the particularity of a place in the making, content and performance of an artwork. By the time the specificity of site in art-making came to be challenged by Miwon Kwon (2004) and others as essentialising and enclosing itself in identity, art walking had already 'moved on' and was carrying its specificities lightly, as much by necessity as self-analysis, but was not yet (or ever) ready to drop them in the flow to globalisation.

The torque enacted on that flow by the spiky particularities of specificity and the anachronistic pace of the pedestrian are together capable of exerting revelatory distortions. Not as some form of localism (which fudges the granularity of specificity into a generality of its own), but by the irritating, eccentric, anomalous, perverse, de-contextualised and non-representative qualities of individual granules (nothing very attractive to the market there), scratched and broken, snagging on the fine weave of smooth space. When understood correctly, this subjecting of the sleek phantoms of the Spectacle to vital, non-human matter's clomping conformism to dull physical 'laws' can bring the occult back into play as a conjuring of spectacular ideology onto matter's lumpy and uneven battlefield. And it is just at the queasy interface of that separation (as much as connection) in the mixture that the spike of specificity can be sheathed in the concerns around side-adaptation that the choreographer and theorist of site dance Melanie Kloetzel is teasing out right now from the most vulnerable of our assumptions about place and performance. Her archaeological excavation of a hidden ideology of adaptation within specificity, and the grand evolutionary and ecologist narratives into which it plugs and from which it is formed, is a warning. To act against these barely visible giants, the Spectacle's trajectories and exchanges can be violently decelerated and redirected; by slowing down light these primitive memes, from somewhere back in the birth of site-specificity, can be persuaded to emerge from the shadows to almost fill the whole arena. The anachronistic objects of non-commodified arts can then serve as useful trip hazards on the Spectacle's superhighways, jutting nails to skewer its memes upon.

Specificity (despite the problems that Melanie Kloetzel and Miwon Kwon have articulated) is also resistant to dominant ideological tropes like "starting again from scratch" and "wiping the slate clean". Walking in specificity, by its inherent and contradictory qualities, when armed with a disruptive Brechtian *verfremdungseffekt*, the "uncovering (making strange or alienating) of conditions... brought about by processes being disrupted" (Benjamin 1973, 18), is more capable than other practico-aesthetic-theoretical activities of attending to and breaking up the slippery spaces of hypermodernity (Augé 1995, Lipovetsky 2005) and tripping up the mobilities paradigm (Urry 2007).

However, there is a danger here. In his *Off the Map* (despite its novelty-like populism, it is a very serious challenge to new walking), writing in broad strokes, Alastair Bonnett upbraids "modern intellectuals and scientists" for "the rise of... the idea of 'space'" at the expense of 'place' (2104, 3), flying in the face of Phil Baker's argument a decade earlier that it was "the 1990s popularity of psychogeography [that] was a last-ditch assertion of place against space" (Baker 2004, 290). For Bonnett 'space' is an accepted and commonly understood concept applicable universally like a Newtonian law; very different to Doreen Massey's "multiplicity... the product of interrelations... predicated upon the existence of plurality... always under construction" (Massey, 9). Bonnett contrasts his 'space' with the specificity of what he calls "real places" (looping back to romanticism and 'authenticity' as privileged by Frédéric Gros), as if certain terrains have perhaps yet to qualify for reality. Which would they be? Refugee camps? Immigration centres? Freeways and globalised production lines? Supermarkets?

Bonnett's "real places", the happy smiling reverse of "non-places", are where "human identity is woven" (2014, 11), places "that allow our thoughts to roam unimpeded" (14); in these "real places" humans make themselves and think themselves, yet there is little sense of the places being made or of Bonnett being part of their making on his visits to them. Instead, these are places that match in stasis and passivity Gros's frozen terrain. In *Off the Map the* specific locations (mostly experienced through a computer screen) evoke a "*genus* (sic) *loci*" (3) that conjures identities, exemplified in Bonnett's odd description of "genuine revolutionaries... bound to place" (205). Extraordinarily, 'Merrie England' has returned, digitally! And the new walking movement will need to be sharp to recognise, expose and oppose its reanimation rising from the ruins of an old psychogeography, just as much as it needs to overleap romanticism and sharpen its wits to changes in the nature of space.

For despite Doreen Massey's warnings about such nostalgic localisms generating "reactionary nationalisms, competitive localism and introverted obsessions with 'heritage'" (1995, 151), there remains something appealing about Bonnett's "real places": their defiance of flow and disruption of smoothness, their making of identities and authenticities in "real places... where people come first" and which "[I]n the face of the flow of modern history... have taken on an oppositional character" (Bonnett 2014 285). In his rhetorical enthusiasm for these authenticities, however, Bonnett manages to tip his whole project into a duality of physical authoritarianism and mental liberality; so that these "real places" emerge, unfortunately, as locations *within* which identities are generated and to which the identities *are then bound*, and yet where somehow *thoughts* are allowed to wander unimpeded. It all sounds suspiciously like a description of the circumstances of a tenured academic (at least, as a tenured academic might imagine them). Rather as Marc Augé's *Non-Places* (1995) reads partly like the travel journal of an international intellectual.

A far better model for the new walking movement for a terrain that is both "real" and fluid are the 'anywheres' of Wrights & Sites: real places found "any where... different from any other where... A utopia that almost exists, wherever you are... it has no flag, borders, position on debt repayment, currency... a meeting of trajectories... where war criminals go when they lose power; why should they be so lucky?... It doesn't even almost exist until you move" (2006, 110-1).

Yes, we are back to space wars; struggles over the very "real" places where very "real" people and their identities and thoughts are bound, impeded, and worse. There is a great sadness here: by first de-prioritising the details and textures of wandering and now absenting himself almost entirely from them, Alastair Bonnett has disqualified himself from finding the very "real" he seeks, excluding himself from the prescription for dis-alienation and the reconciliation of representation to the very "[R]eal conditions of existence" that he apparently seeks and for which the conditions *in practice* seem at last to be emerging: "the practical reconquest of a sense of place and the construction or reconstruction of an articulated ensemble which can be retained in memory and which the individual subject can map and remap along moments of mobile, alternative trajectories" (Lefebvre 1991b, 51).

The new walking movement must not make the same mistakes, nor be swayed by them. Immersed walking practitioners require neither an essentialist conception of place nor an idealist conception of thought. By necessity walkers have always had to process the intense specificity of textures and signs with the motion and transience of their own mobility; a slipperiness which renders them not immune to, but at least prepared for and ready to deploy or take advantage of, the subtle adaptations of specificity and site illuminated by Melanie Kloetzel in recent talks (2014) in Winchester and Plymouth. This is not to say that walking practitioners have not sometimes essentialised and fixed their routes and vistas or idealised and dislocated their thoughts transcendentally, but rather that we need not. That, unlike the sedentary academic, the walker-thinker-journeyer-maker is corporeally and continually provided with the dynamic affordances and inconveniences of specificity and transience, and contradictory mixtures of both.

So let us be clear that the dispirited *genii loci* and cursory *dérives* of the 1990s were not a failure of specificity in itself, but the result of particular walkers adopting far too narrow a frame ("seeing very little") for what that specificity (in all its multiplicity, in any space) could be; adopting far too unambitious and strict a restraint on how compromisingly site-adaptive their documentations and souvenirs could be. Nor was it a failure of mobility, but rather the consequence of those walkers' embrace of an iconoclasm that did not allow for these journeys to become performance-like and performative. Key to both these shortcomings was a 'research' model, lifted wholesale from the situationist project, that assumed that its drifters were discovering a city that was already there, a hidden labyrinth that was passively or seductively awaiting certain walkers of privileged status to unlock it by their understanding and boldness. Rather than taking part in the de-composing and re-composing of the city, changing the city as they re-explored it, their model for revolutionary research tended to reproduce it: "[S]even middle class white males" (Boyle 1998, 89) "seeing very little".

By bringing an understanding of post-dramatic performance to such walking we begin to see that part of the problem, a problem we have not solved yet, is 'walking' itself. A 'walking' that takes no account of those who cannot or do not or who refuse to walk, including the very young, the injured, the reclusive, the excluded, the confined.

When I was 14 I performed or suffered (I was not and am not sure which) a breakdown of some kind; a still theatre that did the trick for me. I became immobile and had to be lifted from my school desk and carried to a car. I was taken to my Nan's sofa and there I lay for four weeks. There was nothing 'wrong' with me, I just needed to not move, or not to move. I got up when I was ready to move again.

We do not have to move all the time – though some, like security guards in shopping malls and employers will argue otherwise when we deploy our "I would prefer not to" – even as nomads. Indeed even as nomads we can leave or drop out of nomadism in order to return to walking that is once again a choice, a rebellion, an anomaly, a nomadism.

This is the precious thing that a Fortean philosophy (Fort 2003) gives us: the refusal to ignore and the permission to embrace anomalies rather than probabilities, and the duty to query 'universals'. If we proceed from anomaly rather than universality or probability, seeking neither a supernatural Big Other nor a positivist materialism, but a 'weird realism' (Harman 2012), then the invitation to us is not to "leave your bed and walk" but to "pick up your bed and walk". In other words, we should take an anomalous stillness with us in mobility; walk as, and in relation to, supine, "horizontal and impulsive" (Land 2011, 501) selves. Each new step a fall or a stumble that can be caught up, recovering, in dancing.

The post-dramatic is partly a "de-hierarchization of theatrical means' (Lehmann 2006, 86) and 'the decomposition of the human being... [that] balances between a metamorphosis into a dead exhibition piece and... self-assertion as a human being... returning to things their value and to the human actors their experience of 'thing-ness'" (165). The post-dramatic is one way of understanding that there is nothing natural or universal about walking; every aspect of it is in question, including an "emphasis on an anonymous and generic type of 'ordinary hero' and 'walker' [who] neglects the specific identities through which people negotiate their passage in the city" (Pinder 2005, 402). Under challenge is the very idea that there is a normal and ubiquitous behaviour – walking – in which we are all engaged and which therefore gives a universal legitimacy and a level playing field to all our walks. There is no such thing: walking "is in no way a technique that will guarantee access to – and equal exchange within – the public sphere" (Pope, 2014, unpaginated), rather, each walk is performative; an enactment in relationship to an illusion of normalcy, to threat, to inhibition, to disability, to appearance, to signs, in which the meaning of "walk" is reinvented and within which the conditions of repression and exclusion are enacted and reinforced whenever resistance to them is not explicitly and structurally inscribed in an anti-walk in the walk.

If we do not resist the universality of walking we condemn ourselves to never finding out how different it can be.

So, while fantasising a walk that is a structural overthrowing of social relations by what it discovers about the city (or whatever site), radical walking will be just as, and more, effectively disruptive when it simultaneously challenges itself and its own structural assumptions and addresses "the particular crisis of bipedal erect posture... [E]rect posture and perpendicularization of the skull is a frozen calamity" and identifies, even embraces, "[N]umerous trends in contemporary culture [that] attest to an attempted recovery of the icthyophidian or flexomotile spine: horizontal and impulsive rather than vertical and stress-bearing" (Land 2011, 501). The crawling performances of Gail Burton, William Pope L. and Veronica Cordova de la Rosa and the falling performances of Amy Sharrocks show us the way.

There is no reason why we, fictional 'leaders' and never followers of a new walking movement, the 'new psychogeographers', cannot meet this challenge in the specificity of the public spaces we seek to change, assaulting the normalising assumptions about what is an acceptable passage through these spaces by addressing the specific inequalities in our assumptions about the pedestrian act, opening up a new and wider range of possible trajectories.

Photo: Kris Darby

Let us stumble as we mean to go on.

finally: what the Laura said

I have told you what Gros and Bonnett did to decompose my walking world, but not what Laura Oldfield Ford said. It is time to correct that, end this book, get away from this pc and walk.

It was an offhand remark, during the *Art of the Edgelands Symposium* (Exeter, UK, 2014); prefacing her presentation, Ford tried to summarise succinctly her relation to psychogeography, starkly contrasting her art practice – emanating from a milieu of squatting emptying inner-city London estates, raves and street resistance – to the "coffee table" books of Will Self.

I was troubled by that. Will Self and Iain Sinclair (the latter of whom has not made his cause any easier by participating in an online advertisement for Audi cars) have become something of a useful shorthand for a 'mainstream psychogeography' against which those who believe themselves more radical can quickly self-define (and I have done it). I was even more troubled when I found Ford herself upbraided online, by neo-situationists The Monstrous Bastards, for quoting the wrong people (Deleuze, Agamben, Ballard) in her work, for deploying a "docu-fiction" that messes with historical fact – "you simply don't know where you are" (!) – and for covering up her MA with "a fair dose of pretend – as well as real – street cred", complaining that Ford's *Savage Messiah* zines are not only "jam-packed with artefact" ready for an appropriating gallery system, but in their collective publication by the academic leftist Verso have become (and here the characterisation is almost identical to the one Ford used against Self) "a trendy Verso book...

death knell of halfway radicalism" (The Monstrous Bastards, 2012, unpaginated).

I went away and read Laura Oldfield Ford's *Savage Messiah* (2011). It is a sophisticated collection of zines under a single cover. Its raw anger at the alienation of communities and individuals is fuelled by feelings, rushes, love, desiring, dreaming and the erotic urge to fight back. Ford uses everyday working materials such as biros and the informal medium of the zine, while deploying a range of literary and philosophical references, rescuing architectural and literary modernism from a blizzard of toothless and fashionable *détournements*. Her hybrid images are complex constructions; their multiplicity defies any single reading, her presence is ambiguous; she comments passionately, she refuses to comment; she protects her interiority while exercising her self-determination.

Though her zines speak of the spontaneity of parties and protests, of self-questioning and heightened states, they are also very aware of themselves as parts of a genealogy of political art. Her drift away from authenticity is a retreat from the state, from the threat of dependency on anything other than her own autonomy. There is no clear meta-narrative in *Savage Messiah*, but, instead, narratives of creeping corruption and authoritarianism, brutalist architecture as playground and battleground (Ford is an inveterate *dériviste*), the redundancy of progressives and the joy of invasive species. Slipping from author/artist into the undifferentiated subjectivity of the text there slowly emerges a kind of composite "I", male and female, a fuzzy waking consciousness punctuated by sharp chemical highs, prefigurative and tough.

More than anything I have written here, Laura Oldfield Ford prefigures what an engaged and vividly serious and sensitive and sophisticated and historically aware and reflexive walking might be. But I would not have found my way to her work (sitting, for the last two years only barely skimmed, on my bookshelf) if it had not been for her swipe at Self. I hope that you, readers and walkers, will likewise forgive and respond to my swipes at Gros, Bonnett, Knowles, *et al*. Not as controversies worth a second thought, for here we "can neither stand nor lie nor sit", but as a good excuse to make your own walkings and watchings and readings and thinkings and to take the next steps to an unpredictable movement.

references

Allen, Jess (2010) *tilting@windmills,* Jess Allen

Andreotti, Libero & Costa, Xavier (1996) *Theory of the Dérive and other situationist writings on the city,* ACTAR

Anon. (1981) 'The Counter-Situationist Campaign In Various Countries' in Knabb (1981)

----- (1985) '36 rue de Morillons' in *Potlach 1954-1957,* Editions Gérard Lebovici

Armitage, Simon (2012) *Walking Home: travels with a troubadour on the Pennine Way,* Faber & Faber

Ashley, Tamara & Kenyon, Simone (2007) *The Pennine Way: The Legs That Makes Us,* Brief Magnetics

Augé, Marc (1995) *Non-Places: an introduction to the anthropology of supermodernity,* Verso

Baker, Phil (2004) 'Secret London: Psychogeography and the End of London' in Kerr, Joe & Gibson, Andrew (eds.), *London From Punk to Blair,* University of Chicago Press

Barber, Stephen (2014) *Performance Projections: film and the body in action,* Reaktion Books

Bayfield, Roy (2010), *Bypass Pilgrim,* trans-genre books

Benjamin, Walter (1973) *Understanding Brecht,* trans. Stanley Mitchell, New Left Books

----- (1999) *The Arcades Project,* trans. Howard Eiland & Kevin McLaughlin, Harvard University Press

Berardi, Franco "Bifo" (2012) *The Uprising: On Poetry and Finance,* Semiotext(e)

Best, Anna (2003) *Occasional Sights – a London guidebook of missed opportunities and things that aren't always there,* The Photographer's Gallery

Bhahba, Homi (1994) *The Location of Culture,* Routledge

Bonnett, Alastair (1996) 'The Transgressive Geographies of Daily Life',

Transgressions: A Journal of Urban Exploration, 2/3. Aug. 1996, 20-37

----- (1998) 'Editorial' in *Trangressions: A Journal of Urban Exploration*, Transgressions

----- (2009) 'The Dilemmas of Radical Nostalgia in British Psychogeography', *Theory, Culture & Society*. Vol.26 (1): 47-72

----- (2014) *Off The Map*, Aurum Press

Boyle, Roger (1998) 'Darton, Pontefract and Beyond: An Exploration by Rail', *Transgressions: A Journal of Urban Exploration*, Spring 1998, 84-9

Bracewell, Michael & Linder (undated) *I Know Where I'm Going: A Guide to Morecombe & Heysham*, Book Works

Brennan, Tim (1999a) *Prospectus: a manoeuvre*, Norbury Park and Landscape project.

----- (1999b) *Guidebook: three manoeuvres by Tim Brennan in London E1/E2*, Camerawork.

----- (2002) *Monograph: Tim Brennan*, information as material

----- (2011) *Enchiridion: three manoeuvres by Tim Brennan in NE Scotland*, information as material

Bridger, Alexander John (2013) 'Psychogeography and feminist methodology', *Feminism & Psychology*. 23 (3) 285-98

Burch, James (1995) 'An Account of Some Experimental Dérive in Newcastle', *Transgressions: A Journal of Urban Exploration*, Summer 1995, 29-32

Careri, Francesco (2002) *Walkscapes*, Editorial Gustavo Gili

Chatterton, Paul (2012) 'Nine principles for reclaiming the good city' in Miles, Malcolm & Savage, Jennie (eds.) *Nutopia: a critical view of future cities*. University of Plymouth Press

Chtcheglov, Ivan (Gilles Ivain) (1953) 'Formulary For A New Urbanism', in Knabb (1981) 1-8

Cocker, Emma (2011) *Manual For Marginal Places*, Close and Remote

Cocker, Emma; Mellor, Sophie & Poulter, Simon (2011) *Manual for Marginal Places*, Close and Remote

Colquhoun, Jim (2003) *A Company of Vagabonds*, self-published pamphlets, www.bit.ly/walk32

Crab Man (Phil Smith) (2012a) *Counter-Tourism: The Handbook*, Triarchy Press

----- (2012b) *Counter-Tourism: A Pocketbook*, Triarchy Press

Crab Man & Signpost (Phil Smith & Simon Persighetti) (2012) *A Sardine Street Box of Tricks*, Triarchy Press

Cracknell, Linda (2014) *Doubling Back*, Freight Books

Craig, Shea & Wilding, Faith (2005) 'Drifting, Rambling, Vagrancy, Wandering: Spatial Practices From Flânerie to the Dérive', (teaching document, no longer available online)

Cooper, Sam (2013) 'The Peculiar Romanticism of the English Situationists' in *The Cambridge Quarterly*, Oxford University Press

Davies, Dan (2014) *In Plain Sight: the life and lies of Jimmy Savile*, Quercus

Davies, John (2007) *Walking the M62*, Self-published: Lulu

De Certeau, Michel (1998) *The Practice of Everyday Life*, trans Steven Rendall, University of California Press

De Jong, Jacqueline (2011) 'A Maximum of Openness' in *Expect Anything Fear Nothing*, Rasmussen, Mikkel Bolt & Jakobsen, Jakob (eds.), Nebula/Automedia

Debord, Guy (1955/1981) 'Introduction to a Critique of Urban Geography' in Knabb (1981) 8-12

----- (1981a) 'Situationist Theses on Traffic' in Knabb (1981) 69-70

----- (1981b) 'Report on the Construction of Situations (1957)' in Knabb (1981) 25-43

----- (1981c) 'Theory of the Dérive' in Knabb (1981) 62-6

----- (1995) *The Society of the Spectacle,* trans. Donald Nicholson-Smith, Zone Books

Deleuze, Gilles & Guattari, Felix (1988) *A Thousand Plateaus*, (trans. Brian Massumi), Athlone Press

Dickinson, Bob (undated) 'Creatures of the MAP', www.bit.ly/walko18

Dusty Bin (1996) 'Review of London Psychogeographical Association Newsletter and Manchester Area Psychogeographic', *Transgressions: A Journal of Urban Exploration,* 2/3. Aug. 1996

----- (2000) 'Three Psychogeographical Groups: Activities, Websites, Publications', *Transgressions: A Journal of Urban Exploration*, 5

Edensor, Tim (2005) *Industrial Ruins: space, aesthetics and materiality*, Berg

Eno, Brian (1975) *Oblique Strategies* www.bit.ly/walko30

Ford, Laura Oldfield (2011) *Savage Messiah*, Verso

Ford, Simon (2005) *The Situationist International: A user's guide*, Black Dog

Fort, Charles (2003) *The Complete Books of Charles Fort*, Dover Books

Furlong, Lucy (2013) *Amniotic City*, Self-published

Gallagher, John (2014) 'A tour of Google Earth'. *Guardian* newspaper, 19.4.14. p.7

Garrett, Bradley L. (2009) 'Psychogeography', www.bit.ly/walk019

----- (2013) *Explore Everything: place-hacking in the city*, Verso

Glover, Nathan (2014) 'Psychogeography, qu'est que c'est?', *City Paper*, 30.4.14. www.bit.ly/walk020

Gracq, Julien (1985) *The Shape of a City*, trans. Ingeborg M. Kohn, Turtle Point Press

Graham, Stephen (1929) *The Gentle Art of Tramping*, Ernest Benn

Gros, Frédéric (2014) *A Philosophy of Walking*, Verso

Haden, David (2011) *Walking With Cthulhu: H. P. Lovecraft as psychogeographer, New York City 1924-26*. (Self-published)

Hancox, Simone (2012) 'Contemporary walking practices and the Situationist International: the politics of perambulating the borders between art and life". *Contemporary Theatre Review*. 22, 2

Hanson, Steve (2004) 'The Art of Navigation', *Street Signs (Spring 2004)* (provided by the author in photocopy)

----- (2007) 'Editorial', *Materialist Psychogeographic Association 1*. (provided by the author in photocopy)

----- (2014) *Small Towns, Austere Times: the dialectics of deracinated localism*, Zero Books

Harman, Graham (2012) *Weird Realism: Lovecraft and philosophy*, Zero Books

Hawkins, Harriet & Lovejoy, Annie (undated), *Insites – a notebook*, Caravanserai

Heddon, Deirdre (2008) *Autobiography and Performance*, Palgrave

Heddon, Deirdre & Turner, Cathy (2012) 'Walking women: shifting the tales and scales of mobility', *Contemporary Theatre Review*, 22 (2)

Hetherington, Kevin (1997) *The Badlands of Modernity: Heterotopia and Social Ordering*, Routledge

Home, Stewart (1991) *The Assault on Culture*, AK Press

Home, Stewart (ed.) (1997) *Mind Invaders: a reader in psychic warfare, cultural sabotage and semiotic terrorism*, Serpent's Tail

Horodner, Stuart (2002) *walk ways*, Independent Curators International

Hughes, Jenny, Kidd, Jenny & McNamara, Catherine (2011) 'The usefulness of mess: artistry, improvisation and decomposition in the practice of research in Applied Theatre' in Kershaw, Baz & Nicholson, Helen (eds.) *Research Methods in Theatre and Performance*, Edinburgh University Press, 186-209

Ingold, Tim (1993) 'Globes and spheres: the topology of environmentalism' in Milton, Kay (ed.) *Environmentalism: the view from Anthropology*, Routledge

James, Mark (2009) 'The Itinerant Toolkit', www.bit.ly/walk024

Jappe, Anselm (1999) *Guy Debord*, trans. Donald Nicholson-Smith, University of California Press

Jenks, Chris (2004) *Urban Culture: Critical Concepts in Literary and Cultural Studies, Volume 2*, Routledge

Jorn, Asger (1985) Helhesten No. 2, cited by Jean-Clarence Lambert, COBRA (1985), Abbeville Press

Kelso, J. A. Scott (1995) *Dynamic Patterns: the self-organisation of brain and behaviour*, MIT Press

Kloetzel, Melanie & Pavlik, Carolyn (2010) *Site Dance: choreographers and the lure of alternative space*, University of Florida Press

Knabb, Ken (ed.) (1981) *Situationist International Anthology*, trans. Ken Knabb, Bureau of Public Secrets

Knowles, Deborah (2009) 'Claiming the Streets: Feminist Implications of Psychogeography as a Business Research Method', *The Electronic Journal of Business Research Methods*, Vol. 7, Issue 1. pp 47-54 www.bit.ly/walk021

Kwon, Miwon (2004) *One Place After Another: site-specific art and locational identity*, MIT Press

LaBelle, Brandon (2012) *Handbook for the Itinerant* www.bit.ly/walk35

Land, Nick (1998 (2011) 'Barker Speaks' in Mackay, Robin & Brassier, Ray (eds.) *Fanged Noumena: collected writings 1987-2007*, 493-506

Lavery, Carl (2005) 'Teaching Performance Studies: 25 instructions for performance in cities', *Studies In Theatre and Performance*. 25 (3) 229-38

Lefebvre, Henri (1991a) *Critique of Everyday Life 1: Introduction*, trans. John Moore, Verso

----- (1991b) *The Production of Space*, trans. Donald Nicholson-Smith, Blackwell

Lehmann, Hans-Thies (2006) *Postdramatic Theatre*, trans Karen Jürs-Mundy, Routledge

Lipovetsky, Gilles (2005) *Hypermodern Times*, Polity Press

Macfarlane, Robert (2012) *The Old Ways: a journey on foot*, Hamish Hamilton

Machen, Arthur (1923) *Things Near and Far*, Martin Secker

Mackay, Robin & Avanessian, Armen (2014) *#Accelerate: the acceleratonist reader*, Urbanomic

MacRae, Jean (1996) 'Two Walking Days' in *Transgressions: A Journal of Urban Exploration*, Issue 2/3, 11-12

MAP (Manchester Area Psychogeographic) (1987) Interview with anonymous MAP member by John Eden, www.bit.ly/walk39

----- (1996) 'From Temple to Fairy Hill' in Manchester Area Psychogeographic 5:4

Marples, Morris (1960) *Shanks's Pony: a study of walking*, The Country Book Club

Marsden, Philip (2014) *Rising Ground: a search for the spirit of place*, Granta

Massey, Doreen (1994) *Space, Place and Gender*, Polity Press

----- (2005) *For Space,* Sage Publications

Mock, Roberta (ed.) (2009) *Walking, Writing & Performance: auto-biographical texts by Deirdre Heddon, Carl Lavery and Phil Smith*, Intellect

Morrison, Ewan (2012) *Tales from the Mall*, Cargo Publishing

Murray, Geoffrey (1939) *The Gentle Art of Walking*, Blackie & Sons

Nawratek, Krzysztof (2012) *Holes In The Wholes: introduction to the urban revolutions*, Zero Books

Nicholson, Geoff (2008) *The Lost Art of Walking*, Riverhead Books

Nold, Christian (2014) *Emotional Cartographies: technologies of the self*, (self-published)

Ono, Yoko (1971) *Grapefruit*, Sphere Books

O'Rourke, Karen (2013) *Walking and Mapping: artists as cartographers*, MIT Press

Orley, Emily (2012) 'Places Remember Events: Towards an Ethics of Encounter' in Andrews, Hazel & Roberts, Les (eds.) *Liminal Landscapes: Travel, Experience and Spaces In-Between* (Routledge, 36-49

Papadimitriou, Nick (2012) *Scarp*, Sceptre

Pearson, Mike & Shanks, Michael (2001) *Theatre/Archaeology*, Routledge

Pile, Steve (2005) *Real Cities: modernity, space and the phantasmagorias of city life*, Sage

Pinder, David (2001) 'Ghostly Footsteps: Voices, Memories and Walks in the City', *Ecumene*, 8 (1)

----- (2005) 'Arts of urban exploration', *Cultural Geographies*. 2005.12. 383-411

Pope, Simon (2000) *London Walking: a handbook for survival*, ellipsis

Radcliffe, Charles (2005) 'Two Fiery Flying Rolls: the *Heatwave* story, 1966-1970' in Rosemont, Franklin & Radcliffe, Charles (eds.) *Dancin' In The Streets! Anarchists, IWWs, Surrealists, Situationists & Provos in the 1960s as recorded in the pages of The Rebel Worker & Heatwave*. Charles H. Kerr Publishing

Rancière, Jacques (2009) *The Emancipated Spectator*, trans. Gregory Eliott, Verso

Rasmussen, Mikkel Bolt & Jakobsen, Jakob (eds.) (2011) *Expect Anything Fear Nothing*, Nebula/Automedia

Rees, Gareth E. (2013) *Marshland: dreams and nightmares on the edge of London*, Influx Press

Richardson, Tina (2013) *Concrete, Crows and Calluses: Dispatches From a Contemporary Psychogeographer*, Particulations

Richardson, Tina (ed.). Forthcoming. *Walking Inside Out: contemporary British psychogeography*, Rowman & Littlefield

Rose, Gillian (1993) *Feminism and Geography: The Limits of Geographical Knowledge*, Polity Press

Ross, Kristin (1996) 'Streetwise: the French invention of everyday life', *Parallax* #2, February, pp. 67-75

Sadler, Simon (1998) *The Situationist City*, MIT Press

Self, Will (2007) *Psychogeography*, Bloomsbury

Shehadah, Raja (2007) *Palestinian Walks*, Profile Books

Shepherd, Nan (1977/2011) *The Living Mountain*, Canongate

Sinclair, Iain (2002) 'City Brain: Iain Sinclair, An interview with Mark Pilkington and Phil Baker', *Fortean Times*, April 2002

Skoulding, Zoe (2012) 'Cathedrals of sand: textual cities' in Miles, Malcolm & Savage, Jennie (eds.) *Nutopia: a critical view of future cities*, University of Plymouth Press

Smith, Phil (2003) 'A Short History of the Future of Walking', *Rhizomes* 07. Fall, 2003, www.bit.ly/walk022

----- (2010a) *Mythogeography*, Triarchy Press

----- (2010b) 'Tourists/terrorists: useful ambiguities in a search for models', *Rhizomes* issue 21, www.bit.ly/walk023

----- (2012) *Counter Tourism: The Handbook,* Triarchy Press

----- (2014a) *On Walking... and Stalking Sebald*, Triarchy Press

----- (2014b) *Enchanted Things*, Triarchy Press

Solis, Julia (2013) *Stages of Decay*, Prestel

----- (2005) *New York Underground: the anatomy of a city*, Routledge

Solnit, Rebecca (2000) *Wanderlust*, Viking Penguin

Sonderman, Bryan (2012) *Walking Games* www.bit.ly/walk34

Stone, Tom (2011) *Where to? From what? A (non, un, mis) guide for escape(ism) and distraction* (self-published)

The Geography Collective (2010) *Mission: Explore*, The Can of Words Kids Press

The Monstrous Bastards (2012) 'Origins and Reflections on the Crap Surrounding an Aestheticised, Lowest Common Denominator, Mass-Marketed, Neo-Psychogeography www.bit.ly/walk37

The Urban Research Group (1998) 'Glasgow 1997, South Africa, 1900. The Event of the Year: Psychogeographers in Sensational Co-incidence', *Transgressions: A Journal of Urban Exploration,* 4, Spring 1998, 77-83

Tompsett, Fabian (1995) 'Society of the Spectacle', *Transgression*, 1, Summer 1995, 81-5

Townley, Anna & Bradby, Lawrence (2005) *Sweep and Veer*, Sideline Publications

Trotsky, Leon (1973) *1905,* Pelican

Urry, John (2007) *Mobilities*, Polity Press

Walkowitz, Judith R (1992) *City of Dreadful Delight: Narratives of Sexual Dangers in Late-Victorian London*, University of Chicago Press

Wark, McKenzie (2011) *The Beach Beneath The Streets: the everyday life and glorious times of the Situationist International*, Verso

----- (2013) *The Spectacle of Disintegration: situationist passages out of the 20th century*, Verso

Wells, H. G. (1938) *World Brain*, Methuen

Whitehead, Simon (2006) *Walking to Work*, Shoeless

----- (2007) *Lost in Ladywood*, Shoeless

Wilkie, Fiona (2014) *Performance, Transport and Mobility*, Palgrave Macmillan

Williams, Alex & Srnicek, Nick (2014) '#Accelerate: Manifesto for an Accelerationist Politics' in Mackay, Robin & Avanessian, Armen (eds.) *#Accelerate: the accelerationist reader*, Urbanomic, 347-62

Wilson, Elizabeth (1991) *The Sphinx In The City*, University of California Press

Wilson, Robert Anton (1978) 'Introduction' in Wilgus, Neil, *The Illuminoids: Secret Societies and Political Paranoia*, Sun Publishing, 8-12

Wrights & Sites (2003) *An Exeter Mis-Guide*, Wrights & Sites

----- (2006) *A Mis-Guide To Anywhere*, Wrights & Sites

----- (2013) *4 x 4 Screens*, Live Art Development Agency

About the Author

Dr Phil Smith is a prolific writer, performer, urban mis-guide, dramaturg [for TNT Munich], counter-tourist, drifter, artist-researcher and academic. He has written or co-written over one hundred professionally produced works for a wide range of British and international theatres and touring companies, and has created and performed in numerous site-specific theatre projects, often with Exeter-based Wrights & Sites, of which he is a core member [**www.mis-guide.com**]. He has collaborated recently with choreographers Melanie Kloetzel, Siriol Joyner and Jane Mason on performances and explorations.

He is Associate Professor (Reader) in the School of Humanities and Performing Arts at Plymouth University.

Phil has published papers in *Studies In Theatre and Performance*, *Performance Research*, *Cultural Geographies*, and *New Theatre Quarterly* and co-authored a range of Mis-Guides with the other members of Wrights & Sites. He has written or co-written a number of other books including: *On Walking*; *Enchanted Things*; *Mythogeography: A Guide to Walking Sideways*; *Counter-Tourism: The Handbook*; *A Sardine Street Book of Tricks*, *Walking, Writing & Performance* and the novel *Alice's Dérives in Devonshire*.

www.triarchypress.net/smithereens

About the Publisher

Triarchy Press is an independent publisher of alternative thinking (altThink) about government, finance, organisations, society, movement, performance and the creative life.

www.triarchypress.net